Brave Arizonans

"Sustaining our democracy depends on public servants courageously upholding the law. Nancy Marshall's book is a timely reminder of this vital point and the brave Arizonans who defended the outcome of the 2020 election in the face of unprecedented attacks."

—**Scott Bales,** Arizona Supreme Court Justice (Retired)

Testament to Integrity

"During a tumultuous time in our country's history, we were subjected to an egregious attempt to circumvent our national election and democracy. Nancy Hicks Marshall has done an excellent job of laying out all the facts about the effort to steal the 2020 election. Additionally, she explains the election process in simple terms.

"I have participated in elections as a voter, poll worker, campaign manager, and candidate for over forty years. However, I never fully understood the details, security measures, and certifications that every election process undergoes to ensure a fair, secure, and transparent election. This book is both readable and educational; it certainly highlights how a small group of dedicated public servants stopped a corrupt few.

"Regarding the six who stopped the steal, I know them all and call several of them my friends. I served with several as a Phoenix City Councilman, worked with them all as elected officials, and represented one as a constituent in my city council district. After reading their stories and getting to know them personally, I understand their integrity and the courage they mustered to stand their ground. They are all a testament to strength, honesty, and integrity. It is no surprise to me that these six stood up for our Constitutions—United States and Arizona.

"Thank you all for your leadership in defending our democracy. God bless you all!"

—**Claude Mattox,** Phoenix City Council (2000-2012)

True Patriots

"Nancy Marshall brings to life the service and dedication of six men who stared down political pressure and threats to uphold their oaths and duties to the Constitution of the United States. These patriots remind us that our democratic values are self-sustaining—our democracy can only flourish thanks to the hard work of men like these."

—**David J. Becker**, Executive Director and Founder
The Center for Election Innovation & Research
@beckerdavidj.bsky.social & linkedin.com/in/davidjbecker

Integrity and Courage

"When Donald Trump attempted to stay in office despite losing the 2020 election, the election results in Maricopa County, Arizona, became the epicenter. There was a fusillade of false claims, political intimidation, and physical threats. Six local political leaders, acting with integrity and courage, ensured that the truth prevailed. This book tells their story. It is a story that deserves, and needs, to be remembered and honored."

—**Robert Robb**
Former *Arizona Republic* columnist, who now writes on *Substack*

Riveting

"At a time of severe political polarization, Nancy Marshall's *Six Who Stopped the Steal* is extremely timely and important. She documents how Republican officials in Maricopa County, Phoenix, worked tirelessly to ensure a constitutional and lawful election despite furious reproach from the far-right. A riveting book based on extensive research of real events, Marshall's book is essential to our understanding of what happened in the 2024 election."

—**Jon Talton,** jontalton.com
Phoenix historian and author of *A Brief History of Phoenix,*
the Phoenix-centric *David Mapstone Mysteries,*
the thriller *Deadline Man,* and the *Cincinnati Casebooks*

A Solid Foundation for True Leadership

"The repercussions of the 2020 Presidential election are still with us. In her book, *Six Who Stopped the Steal,* Nancy Marshall recounts the story of that election and how it played out in Arizona. The heart of the drama rests with six Arizona leaders who stood their ground against tremendous pressures and procedural moves from Republican leaders to delegitimize the winning vote, which, in fact, legally favored the Democrats. Their childhood backgrounds serve as examples of how a solid foundation in values of integrity, kindness, and independent thinking can withstand such pressures and lead to true leadership that prioritizes truth above party and partisanship."

—Alice Stambaugh
Past President, League of Women Voters of Arizona

Remarkable

"In this time, when Trump 47 is actively working to rewrite history, Nancy Marshall has done a remarkable job in *Six* of showcasing the elaborate steps of our election process that prevent fraud while also profiling the courage of six elected officials. Especially noteworthy are the five Republicans who stood up for electoral integrity, despite having voted for Trump and feeling intense pressure from Trump or his allies to overturn the 2020 Arizona Presidential Election result."

—David Wells, GrandCanyonInstitute.org

Fascinating Portrayal

"In *Six Who Stopped the Steal*, the reader will gain an inside look at six individuals, their backgrounds, and the life-altering events of a crucial election and its aftermath. This book is fascinating in its portrayal of these courageous men and the consequences they, and their families, faced—a must-read for those who appreciate integrity and truth."

—Helen Purcell, Maricopa County Recorder (1989-2016)

Upholding the Values of a Democratic Society

"Six individuals can make a tremendous difference in upholding the values of a democratic society. Nancy Marshall's book explores the backgrounds of six Arizona men who courageously stood up to the onslaught of vicious and unfounded attempts to overturn the results of the November 3, 2020, election.

"In an effort to avoid an extra, unnecessary audit, all six men attempted to convince their Arizona State Legislative colleagues, by personal meetings, conversations, and evidence from reports and independent audits, that the Board of Supervisors was in full compliance with all election certification procedures. They were not successful.

"Nancy's narrative describes the intersecting components of the often complex and confusing election process in a very understandable fashion. As she shows us the inner workings of election operations, we gain greater confidence both in the process itself and the fact that our votes really do count. "This book is a fascinating read for all who are committed to ensuring that our elections are run safely and free of lies and untruths."

—**Shari Capra,** Attorney/Mediator

Remarkable Private Interviews

"Nancy Marshall has assembled a fulsome historical record that includes voluminous public sources and remarkable private interviews with officials caught in the center of the (fraudulently manufactured) disputes over the 2020 presidential election in Maricopa County, Arizona. Americans like to think the worst of politicians; we love democracy, but the actual messy nature of politics somehow repels us. Nancy gets unguarded, honest reactions from politicians who responded to threats and misinformation with patience, decency, integrity, and, most of all, honesty. Her book will be a valuable resource to students, historians, and psychologists for years to come."

—**Sam Coppersmith,** Former Member of Congress, former Foreign Service Officer, and international election observer with the National Democratic Institute and The Carter Center

SIX
WHO STOPPED
THE
STEAL

Nancy Hicks Marshall

Nugget Press
Phoenix, Arizona

Nugget Press
Phoenix, Arizona
www.nuggetpress.com

ISBN: 979-8-9939012-1-3 Paperback
ISBN: 978-0-9828259-9-0 eBook
Library of Congress Control Number: 2025923868

Editor: Lynn Thompson, Living on Purpose Communications
Cover Design: Spotlight Publishing House
Interior Design: Marigold2K
Author Photograph: Vance Hicks Marshall

This book is sold with the understanding that neither the author nor the publisher is rendering any form of advice and is based solely upon the author's personal experience. The author and/or publisher shall have neither liability nor responsibility to any person or entity with respect to any loss or damage caused or alleged to be caused, directly or indirectly by the information contained in this book.

Disclaimer: All of the websites included in the citations were accessed prior to November 1, 2025, with no guarantee of accuracy or longevity. Some links that are no longer available may have been archived or deleted.

Publisher's Cataloging-In-Publication Data (Provided by Cassidy Cataloging Services, Inc.)
Names: Marshall, Nancy Hicks, 1941- author.
Title: Six who stopped the steal / Nancy Hicks Marshall.
Description: Phoenix, Arizona : Nugget Press, [2026] | Includes bibliographical references.
Identifiers: LCCN: 2025923868 | ISBN: 9798993901213 (paperback) | 9780982825990 (ebook)
Subjects: LCSH: Gates, Bill, 1955- | Hickman, Clint. | Gallardo, Steve. | Sellers, Jack. | Bowers, Russell. | Boyer, Paul. | Elections--Corrupt practices--United States. | Presidents--United States--Election--2020. | Election law--United States. | COVID-19 Pandemic, 2020-2023--Political aspects--United States. | BISAC: POLITICAL SCIENCE / Civics & Citizenship. | POLITICAL SCIENCE / Political Ideologies / Democracy. | POLITICAL SCIENCE / Political Process / Political Parties.
Classification: LCC: JK1994 .M37 2026 | DDC: 324.660973--dc23

Printed in the United States of America

DEDICATION

To all the election officials and poll workers who
contribute their skill and dedication to make our elections
safe, private, fair, and accurate
in Maricopa County
and
the United States of America

CONTENTS

PREFACE

I undertook this project out of a deep revulsion at the dreadful treatment that six Arizona men received for sticking to their conscience. Rusty Bowers, a Republican and Speaker of the Arizona House of Representatives, said of then-President Trump, "I won't break the law for him." Five others did likewise, and had their lives threatened. Luckily, each of the six agreed to talk with me about what in their youth led them to want to become—to be—men of integrity. It probably helped that I made a solemn promise to each man that I would not twist their words or stories for some other agenda. I am profoundly honored that they have shared significant moments from their lives.

Have you ever encountered someone who said, "I won't read that. I know I don't agree with it." They closed their minds to new perspectives. They faced "cognitive dissonance" with a decided rejection of any new information "monster." Others, when shown flaws of Mr. Trump, have responded with "confirmation bias": "God has often chosen flawed men for His purposes." They acknowledge new information ("Trump has serious flaws"), but confirm that to support him is good because God has chosen other flawed men before. They talk as if we were living 4,000 years ago in an Old Testament theocracy. The Founding Fathers experienced such regimes in England and Europe and rejected them soundly in the First Amendment to the Constitution.

Do you feel safe enough or brave enough to consider the information about the efforts of one man and his allies to steal the election from the verified winner? If so, you will honor the American heritage of upholding our Constitutional principles—and, if necessary, changing your mind in light of the evidence.

Nancy Hicks Marshall
Arizona

INTRODUCTION

What was the steal? How did it get stopped? You've probably heard of the battle cry during the 2020 elections: "Stop the Steal."

The actual steal was something quite different. It was the planned, illegal, and unconstitutional attempt by those who did not want to lose, and then did lose, the election—to prevent the lawful transfer of power or to the rightful winner, Joe Biden.

Six Who Stopped the Steal is the story of six men who learned as boys and young men what integrity meant. Learning this vital life lesson led them to do what was right as adults, at a time and in a place where they faced immense pressure, often with threats to their own lives and to their families. Yet, because of a fundamental quality of character, each one, when called upon, acted with integrity. They examined all the evidence and told the truth.

Integrity doesn't happen in a vacuum. You learn it as a young person and as you grow up. You know you want to be the kind of person who does what's right. So, when the crunch comes, you do. Most of us have had moments when we knew we lacked integrity, or when integrity rose up in us and we did the right thing—sometimes despite temptation or pressure.

Besides telling these stories, I felt we should have a conversation about "Monsters." I hope that by including a short description of what I think a "monster" is—and how we might feel and react to our own "monsters"—we will understand the challenges to our own integrity better as we continue on our path of learning.

Some of the words about elections might seem strange. Refer to the vocabulary list at the end for acronyms such as the BOS and OET, as well as key terms such as audit, canvass, hash code, and Splunk logs.

Now, on to *Six Who Stopped the Steal.*

PART ONE

THE SIX – THEIR YOUTH

"Real Values are not learned. They form.
They form from inside out. They cannot be imposed."

—Alfred K. LaMotte, 1982
from *Plain Living* by Catherine Whitmire

CHAPTER 1

BILL GATES—GRANDPA AND THE GOLF GAME

Grandpa

Born in Rock Springs, Wyoming, in 1971, William Shane Gates (Bill) was an only child who appreciated the presence of his grandfather and parents more than other children might, as they were his primary companions at home. His grandpa, Edgar Terrell, was born in 1922. Grandpa Terrell had only a high school education and became a welder on various projects around the West. Despite his limited education, he constantly read about history and current affairs.

Perhaps it was Grandpa Edgar's stint in World War II that fostered an interest in history and world events. In 1944, when he was fresh out of high school, Edgar was drafted while working at his father's grocery store near Kirksville, Missouri. He did not want to go. There were news reports of thousands of men killed in battle. Still, he understood the essential nature of this war. Hitler was trying to take over Europe and impose a Nazi dictatorship, and was willing to kill millions to do it. He had already taken over France and had been bombing England.

The U.S. fought with the French and English to defeat the Nazi dictator. Edgar shipped out of Boston—and much later, when Bill went to Harvard Law School in Cambridge, Massachusetts, his grandpa joked, "You can see my fingernails scratches in the Boston dock as I tried to hold on and not go to war."

Shortly after D-Day—fateful June 6, 1944, when the Allies shipped thousands of soldiers to land in northern France—Edgar was on a different ship and noted, "I remember the Greek cooks made terrific food." He soon deployed with the Allies to the Western Front (west of Germany, not the Eastern Front, where Hitler fought Stalin and the Soviet Union).

In December 1944, the Nazis mounted a massive offensive in the area from Belgium to Luxembourg on the north coast of Europe, trying to keep the port of Antwerp. Initially, the Nazis had the advantage due to faulty Allied intelligence. Furthermore, the Allies were exhausted from the long battles they had fought to regain control of France, and supplies were scarce. Many men, similar to Edgar, were inexperienced recruits (draftees). It was not an easy situation to turn around.

Nevertheless, Edgar, a member of the Fifth Armored Division of ground troops, understood, as did the other soldiers, that even with inexperience, losses, and lack of supplies during the coldest European winter in decades, he was fighting a military dictator to make the United States—and the world—safe for democracy. The Battle of the Bulge saw some of the heaviest losses of human life of the war. The Nazis suffered 100,000 dead and wounded, and the Allies lost over 8,000 dead with between 65,000 and 85,000 wounded.[1]

Edgar would have seen the true horror of war.

Finally, in January 1945, the Allies prevailed, and from then on, the Nazis retreated. Due to the actions of President Truman in Japan (the Pacific "theater" of World War II)—ordering the atomic bombs to be dropped on Hiroshima and Nagasaki, Japan surrendered, and Edgar was able to avoid fighting there and returned home.

Grandpa Edgar loved to tell stories of the war. He spoke about how he operated a half-track (a small tank), but he was most excited when talking about his time in France after the war. As he noticed young Bill's interest in history, maps, and current events, Grandpa spoke about these topics with his grandson. He was determined to see Bill receive a formal education. "He'd quiz me on everything I read, and if I didn't read something, he'd quiz me on that."

Bill spent a lot of time with his grandpa. Edgar didn't seem to like children much, and he could be grumpy, but after the family moved to Arizona in 1985, he loved to play pinochle at family reunions and at the Recreation Center in Sun City. "Grandpa taught me the finer points of a card game without cheating," said Bill. "He talked many times about how he conducted himself in his work and personal life. He'd say, 'I did the right thing.'"

"And when I would visit with my grandpa, he would quiz me about what I had been reading. Despite his lack of formal education, he was bright and curious. He kept me on my toes. I wanted to learn more, both about cards and about the world around us, and how it worked. That, combined with his work ethic, led me to absorb his message about being honest in all your dealings, whether in cards or in the rest of your life.

"The main influences were my grandpa and both of my parents. I came to understand quite early that honesty and integrity mattered. My mom was born in the midst of the post-war baby boom in 1951. Her mother (my grandmother) was a saint, an incredible mother and housewife. Whip-smart, too! She was also quiet—even if wronged. I believe her silence frustrated my mom, and because of that, my mom always spoke up when she felt she was wronged. She stands up for herself. I took her lesson to heart and have tried to stand up for myself and others when it is necessary. I think that her influence led me to do what I knew was right in the 2020 elections and also to speak out in defense of our election system and the workers who make it run smoothly.

"Dad, who, similar to his dad, didn't have much formal education, served as a project manager for several power plants and eventually became a project manager for nuclear power plants. Even though he lacked the advanced degrees of many of the people he worked with, he got things done. As the political climate regarding nuclear power plants shifted from pro- to anti-, the management of nuclear plant waste storage facilities and safe storage became crucial. He also worked in Utah on the safe storage and disposal of chemical weapons."

There was a time when Bill's dad wouldn't go along with what the boss at the plant wanted him to do.

"Once, when I was in high school, and Dad came home from work, he looked at me and said, 'I told my boss what he needed to hear, not what he wanted to hear.'" Bill's dad got fired. "He held firm with doing the right thing, but it cost him his job."

School

As a child, young Bill attended elementary school in nine different cities across six states. As the new kid in school, his approach was to remain quiet in groups, observing the dynamics of the interactions. "It took me a while to fit in."

Watching and waiting made Bill easy-going and able to get along with a wide range of people, including adults. Talking history and current events with Grandpa Edgar sharpened his mind and his interest in the political world around him. With a natural interest in history, maps, and current events, and Grandpa quizzing him about everything he read, Bill found himself leaning toward the world of law and public service. Politics could be a natural direction.

Grandpa Edgar retired in 1985, and the family all moved to Arizona. Bill attended Deer Valley High School. As a new guy in town, he didn't rush to join the football team or any of the popular kid groups or clubs. After nine different elementary schools, he was cautious about approaching any new surroundings. With public service still a somewhat vague but ongoing thought in the back of his mind, he looked instead to more academic pursuits. One opportunity was a high school mock trial with coaching from actual practicing attorneys, including some trial lawyers. "I started to think of law school and being a lawyer, somehow in public service."

Political activities finally appeared in Bill's life at Deer Valley High when he launched the Teenage Republican Club at the school. "Fate must have had me in its sights. I recently came across a picture from 1988 of a Republican rally attended by Senators McCain and Goldwater. I was wearing a "Keith Poletis" T-shirt. Poletis had resigned as County Recorder to run for County Supervisor. He lost.

Helen Purcell became the County Recorder. She served from 1989 through 2016.

"My parents' and grandpa's determination that I should obtain the formal education that they couldn't have started to take hold. At the same time, I yearned for stability after moving around to so many schools when I was younger." Bill went to Drake University, where he became a state officer of the Iowa Federation of College Republicans and rubbed elbows with Republicans Jack Kemp (who served as U.S. Secretary of Housing and Urban Development under President George H. W. Bush), Phil Gramm (who represented Texas in both the U.S. House and Senate), and Iowa Governor Terry Brandstad.

To Bill, being a Republican in the 1990s and 2000s meant three things: being pro-life, advocating for limited government, and exercising caution in spending. Plus, a fourth: the right of everyone to vote. Bill was the young Republican lawyer recruited to lead the Arizona Republican Party's election integrity efforts during the 2006 and 2008 elections—2008 being the year that Senator John McCain was the Republicans' nominee for President.

Elections confirm the right of every eligible citizen to vote. Learning how to create a system of machines and processes that allows everyone to cast their ballot fairly is essential, whether your political candidate wins or loses. Elections require the support of law and order. To Bill and to Republicans at that time, believing in law and order meant several things. First, it meant catching the criminals and bringing them, with due process and the court system, to justice. Next, it meant upholding the law (and laws) while at the same time working to improve the laws. The 19th Amendment to the Constitution, ratified in 1920, gave women the right to vote, marking a significant improvement. The 1965 Civil Rights Act, which removed legal barriers for Black Americans, was also a better law.

Bill saw himself as an ordinary guy. Having to move around a lot during his elementary schooling years, he had never latched onto a sport other than golf. Bill made the golf team because "they said I had a good attitude." He wasn't the tallest, the handsomest, the most popular, or the captain of the football team. He was not "Mr. Homecoming King." However, he knew how to fit into almost any group, find a place, get along with other students, and, increasingly, get a sense of wanting to become a public servant.

Bill must have done quite well at Drake University in Iowa, because he went on to Harvard Law School, a notable achievement for a young man whose family had not graduated from college. Then Bill returned to Arizona to stay.

The Golf Game

There was always this thing about honor—about doing the right thing even when no one was looking. As a teen—similar to most—Bill sometimes wanted something that wasn't the right thing. "Once, when I was fourteen, my dad and I were playing golf at the Continental Country Club in Flagstaff. It was one of those cool sunny days in the Flagstaff summer when we had escaped from triple-digit Phoenix for a few days in the pines. After Dad had taught me to play a few years before, we had played dozens of times together, and I thought I was pretty good. I wanted to beat him. Thinking back, I think every guy at fourteen wants to beat his dad at something.

"We were on the ninth hole. I remember, because things had been going along pretty smoothly. Not too many bogies, not too many shots into the rough or sand traps. But on this particular hole, I'd gotten myself off the fairway into the rough, behind a tree. I did not have a clear shot at the green. So, not thinking much about it—and definitely not thinking that my dad was watching me—I chipped the ball with my sneaker from behind the tree to a spot where I could at least take a good shot with an iron and get back onto the fairway, with a good chance of landing close to or even on the green.

"We finished up on the hole. Dad had gotten a six, two over par, with an unlucky putt. I had actually hit the ball six times, which was equal to Dad if you didn't count the little kick with the side of my foot out from behind the tree. Dad asked me what score I had made. I lied. I said I had made a six. I thought he hadn't seen me, and I could get away with it.

"But Dad stopped me right there and read me the riot act. We had 'the talk,' the talk about integrity, and *always* doing what was right, even when no one was looking. I had to keep score accurately. It was a matter of honor. We hardly said a word during the entire back nine, but his words bored into my soul. I was ashamed, and I did not want to bring dishonor to my dad.

"It was just one hole in eighteen. It was such a small thing, but it was immense." By the end of that round of golf, Bill knew that he wanted to be and become a person of integrity in whatever endeavor lay before him.

The Law

As Bill understood it, accepting the results of a valid election and allowing leadership to transition peacefully was part of upholding the rule of law. As it came to pass, the rule of law also meant prosecuting the rioters who wanted to take over the U.S. Government on January 6, 2021, insurrectionists who attempted to prevent the peaceful transfer of power. Prosecuting the individuals in a court of law for committing those crimes was part of upholding the rule of law in our democracy.

The Oath

Being a lawyer carries a particular responsibility, and Bill seems to have "run lightly in this harness." That's a metaphor to suggest that acting with integrity and honor comes naturally to him. It was not difficult for him to follow the appropriate rules.

We all need to know what Bill had in mind when he became a lawyer and then a public servant.

The Rules of the Supreme Court of Arizona include, in the Preamble, some of the following phrases:

> [1] A lawyer, as a member of the legal profession, is an officer of the legal system and a public citizen having a special responsibility for the quality of justice…lawyers should conduct themselves honorably.
>
> [2] (A) lawyer performs various functions… consistent with requirements of honest dealings with others.
>
> [5] A lawyer's conduct should conform to the requirements of the law, both in professional service to clients …and in the lawyer's business and personal affairs. A lawyer should use the law's procedures only for legitimate purposes and not to harass or intimidate others. A lawyer should demonstrate respect for the legal system and for those who serve it, including judges, other lawyers and public officials.
>
> [6] As a public citizen, a lawyer should seek improvement of the law, access to the legal system, the administration of justice and the quality of service rendered by the legal profession…a lawyer should cultivate knowledge of the law beyond its use for clients, employ that knowledge in reform of the law and work to strengthen legal education. In addition, a lawyer should further the public's understanding of and confidence in the rule of law and the justice system because the legal institutions in a constitutional democracy depend on popular participation and support to maintain their authority.[2]

This last phrase, about the legal institutions in a constitutional democracy, would become hauntingly powerful as Bill and other

Maricopa County public officials faced difficulties of immense proportions in the 2020 and 2022 elections.

After law school, Bill returned to Phoenix, where he practiced law for several years.

Finally, he entered public life, first as a member of the Phoenix City Council from 2009 through 2016 and then as a member of the Maricopa County Board of Supervisors from 2017 through 2024.

Upon entering a government position—elected, appointed, or employed—Bill and all his colleagues were required to take the following oath or affirmation:

> I (type or print name), do solemnly swear or affirm that I will support the Constitution of the United States and the Constitution and laws of the State of Arizona, and I will bear true faith and allegiance to the same and defend them against all enemies, foreign and domestic, and that I will faithfully and impartially discharge the duties of the office of [Supervisor of the Maricopa County Board of Supervisors] according to the best of my ability, so help me God (or so I do affirm).
>
> Signed by the official.[3]

Bill embraced this standard of conduct as he entered service as a member of the Maricopa County (AZ) Board of Supervisors.

Bill and his colleagues on the Board of Supervisors were soon to learn how events surrounding the 2020 elections thrust those standards and that oath onto full center stage.

CHAPTER 2

CLINT HICKMAN—DESIGNATED DRIVER

"Why do I try to decide to make honest decisions and do the right thing?" Clint repeats to no one in particular—and to each one of us. "It was my complete family. In the family business, with parents and siblings, if I were not honest, I'd get my butt kicked. If I were not honest, I would let people down."

Clint Hickman was born in 1965 at St. Joseph's Hospital in Phoenix and then lived on the family farm in Glendale.

"My grandma started the family business during World War II, selling from her back porch. She started with fifty laying hens. Neighbors would come around to the back porch and buy her eggs. She would have washed them off so they were ready to use. She wanted to have a business, and she also knew that she wanted people to be happy with her eggs. It went from fifty hens to a huge enterprise. My dad and mom became involved. The business expanded rapidly to become a big chicken farm. Today, there are four farms in Arizona and one in Colorado."

When you live on a farm, you start working and doing chores at an early age. "I have three older brothers, two, four, and six years older than me. When I was about four or five, I remember going with them to the barn at night. The business had become pretty large by then, and we caged our chickens. Some of them would escape. Our job was to enter the pitch-dark barn at night and walk very silently until we'd see a chicken, usually under a cage. The white of its feathers would catch whatever light there was. Then one of my brothers would flash a light in their eyes. Chickens act as though they are deer in the headlights—it's called the 'chicken in the flashlight syndrome.' In that one moment when the chicken didn't move, I would reach under the cage, grab the chicken, and we'd put it back in the cage. I was just the right height to do the job really well.

"We'd catch the chickens by night and then gather eggs by day.

"Why would I be honest? The same reason everyone in my family was honest—Grandma, Mom, Dad. We were producing food that people would eat, and we had to be scrupulously reliable about our product. At first, we knew all our customers personally. How would we feel if we sold rotten eggs and someone got sick? That was unthinkable. You might think it was only eggs, but almost everyone eats eggs. We have always wanted to produce the best and be trustworthy in our dealings.

"As a kid growing up with the family business, I realized that honesty and integrity were standards from more than the business. We were always around Dad's other family members and friends. If you screwed up, you would damage the honor of the family's reputation for decency and integrity. My parents loved my brothers and me, and we loved them. I can't remember ever wanting to hurt my mom or dad or to make them ashamed of me."

As a boy growing up on a farm, Clint learned how to do everything—haul water, repair wagons, fix equipment, and dig ditches. As the youngest of four boys, he got to tag along with his brothers on most of the farm work and other tasks as well. "During the summers, we weren't allowed to sit around inside and watch TV cartoons. Dad said, 'It's okay if you are doing sports. But if you're not at Little League, you need to be working on the farm.' Some of my friends got to watch cartoons, but as a rule, I preferred being out working with my brothers.

"Hanging out with my brothers also helped shape my idea of who I wanted to become. I saw the good they did, and I saw what was not so good. From the time I was about ten, they would take me along when they all went out to the Big Sky drive-in movies at night. They would pick up some girlfriends on Saturday nights. Somehow, there was always a lot of beer. We'd go to the movie, all piled in the truck, and watch age-inappropriate fare. My brothers would drink way too much. The girls would be horrified. Then, at the end of the movie, they made me the designated driver."

Some of the girls considered Clint the "mature" one because he was actually responsible for everyone's safety.

"Since I lived on a farm, I'd been driving a truck since I was eight or nine. But I was seriously underage, so we'd drive the back roads not to get caught.

"On Sunday mornings at breakfast, my parents would ask us all how he evening went and what we did. My brothers would all look at me. I learned quickly how to keep a brother's secrets. I'd shrug. 'Fine,' I'd say. I wasn't going to rat on them and get them into trouble. I didn't want trouble for any of us. Plus, if I ratted on them, my brothers wouldn't take me on the next adventure.

"Anyway, I saw stuff about them, especially the heavy drinking, that I knew I didn't want to copy. However, there were also good things, especially the way they worked on the farm, did their hard jobs well, and took care of problems when needed, which I admired. That's the kind of person I wanted to become."

To Clint, an active Republican party supporter, serving on the Maricopa County Board of Supervisors was a way to offer public service in his community. That was it. He did not intend to use the position, as some do, as a mere stepping stone to a more powerful political office. Clint served on the Maricopa County Board from 2013 through 2024. He took the same oath of office that Bill and the others all took when he was sworn in.

In January 2020, with unanimous agreement from fellow Board members, Bill Gates handed the position of Chairman over to Clint, and he served in that capacity until January 2021.

Little did Chairman Clint Hickman know how dangerous it would become for the Supervisors, their families, their staff, and other election workers when he took the reins as the Board's designated driver.

CHAPTER 3

STEVE GALLARDO—QUIET COMMITMENT

Steve Gallardo is a fourth-generation Arizonan. Born in 1968, he grew up attending public schools in Maryvale. "I was the third of four siblings, with an older brother, older sister, and a younger brother.

"We were definitely a working-class family. My father worked, my mom stayed at home, and we supported the union. We attended church, and everyone had to vote. The vote was necessary.

"Where did a sense of wanting to have integrity come from? Well, Dad was always a straight shooter, did the right thing. More than once, he said, 'Sometimes you may suffer consequences, but you still do the right thing.' I think I got that from Dad."

Steve's father died when he was nine years old. "Mom had to raise the four of us as a single mom. She worked part-time at St. Joseph's Hospital to make ends meet and help all four of the kids have a good life.

"Being nine when my dad died may be how I got the desire to work and influenced my commitment to family. I remember always wanting to work, earn a little money, help my family, and have some things of my own. I rode my bike and had a paper route delivering the *Phoenix Gazette*. As we grew into adulthood, we remained close and caring, and I have become a devoted uncle. I've always lived in the same neighborhood as my mom, because as she gets older, I want to help her out with some chores and shopping for groceries.

"In high school, I played a lot of baseball and soccer, and I was active in student clubs such as MEChA and Student Government. We had a lot of fun, did a lot of volunteer work, and ran fundraisers for good causes. I completed my formal education at Rio Salado Community College.

"I knew from high school that I wanted to be in public service. My dad had always worked hard and volunteered in the community. He was head of our Boy Scout troop for several years. He was always willing to help someone. Being a union member was also part of his desire to support folks within the community, families who were working hard and sometimes struggling to get by.

"So, in 1988, after high school, I started work for the Maricopa County Election Department, working for Karen Osborn and Helen Purcell. I was the Campaign Finance Director and Training Officer for 14 years."

In 2014, Steve resigned from his county job to help political candidates understand the process of collecting signatures and getting on the ballot. He also served on the Maryvale Village Planning Committee, the Governing Board of the Cartwright Elementary School District, and eventually the Phoenix Union High School District.

"There had been a recent redistricting, and my legislative district was predominantly Hispanic. I resigned from the County and ran for the Arizona House of Representatives in Legislative District 13. I served in the House for three terms.

"I live in a mostly Hispanic community. SB 1070 adversely impacted us, being a broad and strict anti-immigration bill passed in 2009. I decided to run for the Arizona Senate and sponsored a bill to repeal SB 1070. We did not succeed that time, but much of that law was struck down as unconstitutional by the federal courts."

Steve had known he was gay from the time he was an adolescent. He had never hidden this aspect of his life, and all his family and friends knew and respected him. But he did not publicize his personal life.

"There came an ugly moment at the legislature in 2014 when the majority in the legislature passed SB 1062, which sought to allow businesses to deny services to LGBTQ people. Governor Jan Brewer vetoed the legislation, but I realized I should take a stronger public stance. When some legislators threatened to 'out' me, I invited some newspeople to a press conference and 'outed' myself.

"That event taught me that there are folks in the legislature who are willing to do some quite mean-spirited things. When my term finished, I chose not to run again." When Mary Rose Wilcox vacated her seat on the Maricopa County Board of Supervisors in 2014, he stood in for that seat, followed by re-election for several terms.

For Steve, canvassing and certifying the 2020 election results was not difficult. The job of the Supervisors was to canvass and certify the election results of Maricopa County. The elections were extremely well run with accurate results.

"I've learned that you sometimes have to suffer consequences, but you should always go with what you feel in your heart is the right thing. We had all taken an oath to uphold the U.S. Constitution, the Arizona Constitution, and the laws of the state. We knew what was right, and it was our job to do it."

CHAPTER 4

JACK SELLERS—THE HAM BONE

"I was born into poverty. My mom gave birth to me in my grandparents' house outside Wichita, Kansas. My family home was a three-room house—not three bedrooms, just three little rooms. There was the kitchen, the living room, and one bedroom.

"My mother was the bedrock of our family. She worked long hours six days a week in the butcher's department of a major grocery store to keep food in the house. I mainly lived with Mom, an older sister, and a younger brother. My mother and father divorced early in our lives. My father died when he was thirty-eight, probably from alcohol.

"I can remember having some job since I was about ten years old. I'd do just about anything. That way, I'd have some money for things I needed or wanted beyond what my single mom could afford to support three kids. One of my first jobs was working at a small local grocery store after school and on Saturdays. I was paid a weekly amount. I don't remember how much, but I was allowed to charge things. So, between candy, pop, and mum's requests for items needed at home, by the end of the week, the store rarely owed me much money.

"Between times, I also sold stuff door to door, such as magazine subscriptions, salve, greeting cards, anything to make a little money.

"When I was sixteen, the grocery chain where my mother worked hired me to work in their produce department. I worked there during my high school years in Kansas.

"I did not like being poor, and I was ashamed of our house and where we lived. When someone not familiar with our neighborhood would offer me a ride home, I'd always have them drop me off a block away so they wouldn't see where I lived."

When Jack went to high school, he didn't do well, with a mom who worked too hard and a dad who was not around. In his junior year, he started hanging around with the wrong guys. "I avoided drinking. I hated what alcohol did to my father, and drugs weren't a thing in my generation in Kansas, but the guys I hung around with drank and frequently got into trouble on purpose. They were aimless and headed in the wrong direction.

"Poor Mom must have been at her wits' end. She had always tried to guide me, encouraging me to do well in school and do the right thing, but I was going off track fast. Early in my senior year, she put her foot down. She sent me to live with my uncle Bob in California.

"Uncle Bob was career military, and the rules were clear. But I really liked living with him. I felt that he cared about me, and expectations were obvious. I got excellent grades in school, almost all As.

"In my Senior year in this new California high school, I was enjoying being a good student and popular with the other students, as well as the faculty. About midway through our semester, the top athlete in the school, who sat across from me in math class, took me aside and said, 'I notice you always finish our tests about halfway through class. Can you slip me enough answers to pass so that I don't lose my eligibility to play sports?'

"I thought, what can it hurt? He wasn't going to learn math regardless, so even though I knew it wasn't proper, I agreed to help. It was so easy, and I was sure no one knew.

"Several weeks later, I was in the hallway outside of class, and a friend asked me how I was doing in math. I was about to answer when the math teacher, who happened to be nearby, said, 'So far, Jack has an A and a C.' He knew what we were doing! The teacher had not called me in to punish me or say anything, and he probably did not punish my classmate, but he had seen me, and he knew. At that moment, I realized what an important value it is to always be honest, even when you think no one is looking!

"The irony was that, despite excellent grades in my senior year, since California had different standards than Kansas, my credits didn't add up to a full four years of high school. So, I did not receive a high school diploma that year, nor did I ever.

"Several of my friends were going off to New Mexico State University on a co-op program. You could work for a semester and then attend school for a semester. Or work mornings and attend school in the afternoons. I wanted to do it. The problem was that I didn't have a high school diploma, so I didn't qualify for entrance.

"Since I didn't get into the co-op program, I looked for a job to save enough money for my first year in college. I worked at a supermarket while living in California. Because of my experience, the manager hired me to manage the produce section. I had to join the union and, since I was the only person in the produce section, I was classified and paid as a department leader. Excellent money for a person right out of high school! I saved enough money by the end of that year to enroll in NMSU for the spring semester.

"A letter from the principal of the high school I attended in California helped get me admitted to NMSU. With that tuition paid, I had no money left at the end of the summer semester.

"That summer was tough, but people were good to me. One time, I went to a café and asked to buy a ham bone. I had some beans, and I thought I could cook them with the bone and get by. The lady asked me how much money I had. 'One-fifty,' I said. She said she could sell me a ham bone for that amount. I took the wrapped package home. When I unpacked the bone, I found that she had included two ham steaks. That was so decent and kind of her. I remembered that kindness till today.

"I met Marie at college. I don't know what she saw in me. I was a poor kid without a high school diploma, and she was a star student with a nice family. They invited me to dinner almost every night, which helped keep costs down. Somehow, Marie and I knew we were meant for each other. When her father had to accept a transfer out of state at the end of the semester, he told Marie she had to go with her family. She said, 'No, I'm staying with Jack.' Two weeks later, we were married. Marie and I were together until her passing in 2012.

"I learned a few more important lessons in college. One day, my history professor, Dr. Garret, walked into the classroom and said, 'John Burns, you're an asshole!' There was a group gasp, and then dead silence in the class. We were shocked. He had never used foul language at all.

"Professor Garrett then said to us, 'You curse once, it has an effect. If you curse all the time, it will lose its effect. Whatever you say, choose your words carefully.' I've never forgotten that. I try to choose my words with care, and I generally don't swear unless I feel I need it for impact!

"Professor Garrett also taught something else. As a white kid from a poor background, growing up with mostly white people, I thought I understood a lot, especially about being poor. One day, when Dr. Garrett was talking about race in class, I said, 'I understand, because I'm poor.' Dr. Garrett handed me a book. It was titled *Black Like Me* by John Howard Griffin. Dr. Garrett said to me, 'All I ask is that you promise to read it.'

"I read that book, and after finishing it, I had a much different perspective. Racism has had a far worse impact on Blacks in this country. I will never assume that I know how it was for Black people, poor or not, just because I grew up poor.

"Another life lesson in college occurred when I served as president of the Blue Key Honor Society. The University Vice President called me into his office. He told me that he wanted his nephew inducted into Blue Key. His nephew's credentials were marginal. After much deliberation, 'we' found a way to induct his nephew. At his first Blue Key meeting, the nephew informed me that Blue Key needed to establish stricter requirements for membership. The lesson? It doesn't pay to compromise your standards simply for political reasons."

Jack and Marie had a baby while in college. She worked full-time so he could go through college more easily, and then it would be his turn to support the family. They shared babysitting and parenting responsibilities. Once he graduated, Jack worked full-time and supported Marie as she finished her teaching degree. She became a school teacher.

Jack earned a B.S. in mechanical engineering. He, Marie, and the family moved to Southern California to work for Shell Chemical. There, he also learned several important lessons about how to live life.

First, when assigned to a project, he needed to take full responsibility for it. That meant he had to know his subject thoroughly and be willing to back it up. He had to believe in it because he was expected to stake his job on his work.

Second, he had to shorten any written proposal to one page. Top management would not take the time to read three pages, and the one page had better be good. "At that time, Marie helped as editor."

The lesson was that when you give people responsibility, you provide them with the authority to get the job done. Jack took on many projects, accepted responsibility, spoke his convictions about what projects needed, and brought success to his company. Over the years, he rose to increasingly responsible positions. He was knowledgeable, honest, and took responsibility for his work. After a couple of years, he came to Arizona to work for General Motors, ultimately becoming the Facilities Manager of the GM Desert Proving Ground in Mesa.

"While at GM, I was asked to be a panel leader at an Arizona Town Hall. I was concerned because it was a topic that I knew well and had strong feelings about. I knew that as a panel leader, my job was to listen to everyone and to find consensus rather than impose my opinion. I found that by listening to all sides of an issue, you can learn even if you are one of the more knowledgeable people in the room on that topic. What a valuable lesson for my later life in politics. You learn by listening rather than by arguing!"

Finally, after retiring from private engineering employment with a deep knowledge of transportation and a long career of getting along with everyone and successfully managing projects, Jack turned to community service. First, he served on the Chandler City Council, and, in 2019, he was appointed to the Maricopa County Board of Supervisors. He was elected to the Board in 2020 and served there until 2024. Jack took the same oath as the others:

> I, (type or print name), do solemnly swear or affirm that I will support the Constitution of the United States and the Constitution and laws of the State of Arizona, and I will bear true faith and allegiance to the same and defend them against all enemies, foreign and domestic, and that I will faithfully and impartially discharge the duties of the office of [Supervisor of the Maricopa County Board of Supervisors] according to the best of my ability, so help me God (or so I do affirm).[4]

With a history of responsible management under his belt and a commitment to honor, Jack arrived at the Board of Supervisors as the 2020 election season—and the COVID-19 pandemic—were about to dominate the headlines.

CHAPTER 5

RUSTY BOWERS—IN A HEARTBEAT

"I am a fourth-generation Arizonan," says Russell "Rusty" Bowers. "My mother was a pioneer in Arizona in 1875. Her father, Benjamin Noble, settled his family in St. Johns, then to Nutrioso, near Springerville." Rusty has deep roots in his beloved state.

Born in 1952, Rusty spent his formative years in Chino Valley, north of Prescott. His father had bought a farm there and worked many jobs to keep the farm in the family. After being embezzled by a business partner, his grandpa moved to California during the Depression. Since Grandpa was saddled with debt, Rusty's father did not have the benefit of family support while working at the Los Angeles Brick Company from the age of fourteen in the 1930s. After serving in the Marine Corps during World War II, Rusty's father moved the family to Arizona and Chino Valley for better opportunities. Farming was never easy, so working extra jobs came naturally.

"We went to a little church in Chino Valley. It was a small LDS church, the Church of Jesus Christ of Latter-day Saints, with a mixture of people, mostly farmers. We were a close community.

"I knew Donetta from childhood, and we married much later. Her father visited us in Chino Valley. He was a man of impeccable character, always honest and ethical, and I admired him from a very young age.

"Both my mom and dad went through the Depression in the 1930s. They worked hard and were used to just getting by. Mom's dad, Parley King, had been in World War I, which had a profound influence on him. WWI was known for its trench warfare. He had saved twenty-seven men by hauling them out of the trenches where they were dying.

"They had all been hit by toxic gas used by the enemy. His lungs were never strong again. Those events affected him for the rest of his life. He was quiet and subdued, with somber memories and serious health issues. I think his experience, along with that of my parents, set a tone in our family of caution, conservative conduct, and scrupulous honesty, with no frivolity.

"Since having the farm in Chino Valley was always a financial struggle, we were expected to do chores at an early age. I remember milking the cows when I was five. The cats would line up on the opposite side of the cow, and I would squirt them in the face, and they would lick off the milk.

"When I was about six, we moved to Scottsdale and went to Scottsdale public schools. By the fourth grade, I was mowing the lawn and trimming the trees. We swam in the Salt River irrigation ditch right in front of our house during the summers.

"I often went to work with my dad from the time I was ten or eleven. My brothers were three and six years older than I was. We all put in a lot of work with Dad, masonry and re-plastering, all over Arizona. In Scottsdale, I would help shovel sand into the dump truck for our father. Then he would drive into Phoenix and sell to MarVel Masonry. Hot summers with a shovel, with a cool canal swim between loads.

"From the outset, Dad set the example, and we understood that it was hard work, and we were doing good, honorable work for honest pay. Every time we went out on a job, I could feel how we were supposed to be of service and be good, honest people. A staple for lunch was graham crackers and milk.

"I was a precocious kid, a little wild, I guess. I loved sports. I was outgoing, enjoyed singing, and loved spending time in the mountains with my brothers. Our dad was both fun and strict. I remember that he wouldn't excuse wrong behavior just because we were away from home.

"This expectation about our behavior played out in several ways. One day, a guy who I thought looked like a hippie flipped me off—gave me the finger. Without thinking, I went over and punched him in the face. He fell to the ground. I had knocked him out. I left him there on the ground and ran home. I knew what I had done was wrong. I was ashamed of myself, and I knew that I had to be brave enough to say I was sorry.

"I knew where he lived, so an hour later, I went to his house and knocked on the door. A big, gruff man answered, who was his father. I could see the kid in the background, lying on the couch. He had a big ice pack up against the side of his face. The father asked in an angry voice, 'Who are you?'

"'I'm the one who hit your son,' I said. 'I came to apologize.' It was hard to do, but it was the right thing to do.

"'Well, you better leave fast,' said the man, 'because I've called the cops.' He was furious, but he let me off the hook. I had a lot to think about from that incident. He had given me a second chance to choose a better path.

"At times, my dad didn't have to say much because his demeanor told me a lot. One time, a friend and I had gone hiking in the Superstition Mountains east of Mesa. There, we came upon a huge stash of many, many boxes of dynamite. We decided to take some. It was just there. So, we took two boxes and drove home.

"But finally, my girlfriend pulled the truth out about my sunburn and said I should take the dynamite back. I guess she had a better conscience than I did. I realized she was right.

"Anyway, I asked my dad to borrow his truck. 'Why?' he asked. 'Because I need to return this dynamite to the Superstitions.' He only said, 'Be careful.'

"Dad had been a munitions expert in the Marines in World War II. When I returned home from returning the dynamite, he asked me about the kind of explosives we had found. I described them, and he pointed out the danger. 'The ones with the white powdery surface could have exploded with the heat of your hand, holding them.'

"Both his quiet affirmation that I had to take the explosives back, and his realization of what I had done, how it could have been a disaster, made me think of doing the right thing in the first place, not to steal, and the need to be more thoughtful. I could have blown us both to smithereens.

"There was another incident when I hit someone. I was in Boy Scouts, and a bigger, older boy was bullying my friend, who was younger and smaller than him. He was making fun of his old, tattered uniform, which made him cry. My friend was a nice kid, but not very strong. I went over and confronted the big guy. 'I don't like bullies,' I told him. 'Pick on someone your own size.'

"He spoke right back at me. 'Gonna make me?'

"I wasn't his size, but I was bigger than my smaller friend. I punched him and knocked him down. I was glad to defend my friend, and the bully never returned to the Boy Scouts. Still, I realized that I was strong and could hurt people, and punching someone was not the right thing to do. Today, I would handle that situation differently, using words, even if he hit me. Afterward, I decided not to use my fists that way anymore. But I still hate bullying."

In high school, Rusty was an all-around guy. He played varsity basketball after a knee injury ended his football-playing career. He sang baritone in the a cappella choir and wound up being the lead baritone at the Arizona All-State Choir. He loved to sing.

Rusty has become a well-known artist in his own right. "I started drawing when I was four or five in the little church in Chino Valley. It continued in Scottsdale at the church near Miller and Earll. My mom always supported my art. She would make a drawing, and then, quietly, have me copy the image. I loved drawing with her, and it kept me moderately quiet."

So, Rusty took art classes in high school. In his senior year, he entered a painting and won the All-State Interscholastic Art Contest. With his artwork shown in the Phoenix Art Museum and in the White House, he knew it was a calling.

After high school, Rusty went on to work in construction, teach art, and produce many fine landscapes and bronze works. Today, his works from the Eddie Basha Art Collection in Chandler are featured in the Western Spirit Museum in Scottsdale.

Finally, Rusty was encouraged to run for the Arizona Legislature as a Republican. He felt led to run as part of his service to his community. There, he learned a hard lesson that telling the truth is not always well received by others, even those who claimed to be friends and allies. Sometimes, telling the truth can become dangerous. Nonetheless, when quizzed about the trouble he faced for his honesty, he said, "I'd do it again in a heartbeat."

CHAPTER 6

PAUL BOYER—THINKING FOR MYSELF

Paul Boyer was born at "Good Sam"—Good Samaritan Hospital—in 1977, in the center of Phoenix.

"I don't remember a lot about my childhood, except that we moved a lot. Every two years, we would move to a new place. The earliest memory I have is of living in a trailer in Camp Verde, AZ, with my older brother, Ben, and both of my parents.

"At some point, we moved to Winslow, AZ, where I learned how to ride a bike, and we had a dog. My dad was the senior pastor at the Baptist church there for a few years. My parents only allowed us to listen to Christian music, so Michael W. Smith and Amy Grant were okay.

"From there, we moved to south Phoenix, where my dad took a senior pastor position at Grace Baptist Church near 40th Avenue and Buckeye. When we first moved into the parsonage, located right next to the church, some local gang bangers sprayed graffiti on the church. My dad reached out to them, played some ball with them at the park, and we never had any problems with them again.

"I always had my older brother and both my parents. They insisted that we go to church every Sunday. Even though the message didn't penetrate my heart at the time, looking back, I am grateful. I heard God's word three times a week, on Sunday mornings and evenings, and Wednesday nights. I would later recall my favorite Bible verses the night God got a hold of me.

"Something I didn't quite realize at the time, but was true, is that since I had a fair amount of time by myself, I was left to figure things out on my own. We moved around a lot. Dad would work at various churches, and when he was not working as a pastor, he worked as a truck driver. Both of my parents worked and were very busy, so I was glad to have time with my older brother.

"I was a pretty good kid. I could have done better academically if my teachers had challenged me more, and I played nearly every sport they would let me play. At Deer Valley High School, I was a member of the wrestling team and participated in the gymnastics class.

"I loved the discipline and training. However, some of the guys on the team would go out after practice, party, and get drunk. That never made sense to me. I always thought, 'Why work so hard in practice and then ruin it all by drinking and being hungover the next day?' I could never stomach the party scene.

"When I turned seventeen, something happened that changed my life. During the summer of 1993, having lived in Phoenix for most of my life, my parents told me we were moving to Tucson. I had visited Tucson and had some friends there, but I did not want to live there.

"So, when I asked when we were moving, they said, 'Tomorrow!' I was entering my junior year in high school, and they were tearing me away from all my friends and everything I knew. I was furious.

"But it was the best thing that happened to me. Since I played sports, I was able to channel all my energy (and anger) into weightlifting, football, basketball, baseball, and track and field. I made friends on different sports teams.

"Joe was one of my classmates. At first, we couldn't stand each other since he was preppy and I was a jock, but we were dating two girls who were best friends. Having to spend time together, we ultimately became best friends as well.

"Joe had been in a car accident in which a girl had died, and he had survived. God used this event to get a hold of him, and Joe ended up surrendering his life to God.

"We went to a Christian school together. Joe was the lead singer in a band that sometimes played in the chapel. Sometimes, at the chapel on Wednesday mornings, Joe would speak about God, and how we all ought to devote our lives to Him. I recall thinking at the time that I had grown up with this message, and I didn't need to hear more of the same from Joe.

"However, one weekend during the summer after our junior year, my life changed. Joe invited me to grab coffee with him. We spent several hours together that evening. He was never 'preachy.' I don't recall anything he said in particular. But I do remember a still small voice convicting me of my sin.

"Although I've never heard the voice of God audibly, I knew God was speaking to me. He was asking me, 'Who are you living for?' I already knew the answer. It wasn't for God. I was living for myself. It was then that God called me out of my sin and to Himself. And I am never more myself than when I am following Him.

"The next year, I went to visit a friend at Calvary Chapel Bible College in the San Bernardino Mountains of California. I loved it there. Although I had never intended to go to a Christian college, I stayed through every single class. I knew after that week that I wanted to attend there."

Due to Paul's financial situation, it took him three years to finish the two-year program. He worked in construction the summer before college, and he worked at the college's youth camp on weekends. It was there that he started to develop his conviction of pleasing God, not man. He remembered Jesus Himself saying, "What does it profit a man to gain the whole world but to lose his own soul?"[5]

"I came to realize that what matters most is not elected office or getting bills passed, important as those things are. It is hearing the words of Jesus Himself saying to me, 'Well done, you good and faithful servant.' That is what ultimately matters."

After attending Bible college, Paul returned to Arizona and enrolled in Arizona State University West, where he obtained a B.A. in English and a Master's degree in Communication Studies. He became a teacher of Latin and in Communications, a profession he continues to this day.

Paul also held a position in communications for the Republican House Majority and worked with all Republican members of the House from 2008 to 2011.

In the summer of 2009, Paul suffered an Arteriovenous Malformation (AVM) that burst in his head, requiring brain surgery. The night before surgery, a friend assisted him in drafting his Power of Attorney and Living Will documents. "I realized then that I could die tomorrow on the operating table." This awareness gave Paul a newfound appreciation for life.

Three years later, Paul became a state legislator, serving in the Arizona House from 2013 to 2018. He then became his district's state Republican senator. In 2019, Paul took on his own party, working to pass a law that would allow adult victims of child sexual abuse to file a claim in court against their abusers up until their 30th birthday—a significant improvement over the previous time limit of having to sue by their 21st birthday.

That was not the first time Paul took a position different from his Republican colleagues. Nor would it be the last. When confronted with the 2020 election "monster," he encountered a controversy he had not expected. Again, Paul would have to think for himself.

PART TWO

THE FOUR MONSTERS OF 2020

"Humans struggle to hold two seemingly opposing ideas in the heads at the same time. We like a simple answer, and we like a fall guy. Add in politicians' rhetoric, the fact that most people's eyes glaze over…and you have a perfect storm of misunderstanding."

—Joan Meiners,
Arizona Republic, August 3, 2025

"Oh, hello. It's you again.
"Thanks for showing up. For making me so alert.
"But I see you.
"You're no monster to me."

—Michelle Obama
The Light We Carry: Overcoming in Uncertain Times

CHAPTER 7

WHAT IS A MONSTER?

What—in this book of ours—is a "monster"? And why are we talking about it?

Here's what I believe. "Monster" is a metaphor for something too big and scary for us to cope with easily. It doesn't have scales and breathe flames, but it can overwhelm us. Depending on whether we feel safe or not, we may deal with the "monster" or we may avoid it. If we feel safe learning about something new, we will learn. If we don't feel safe, we have to feel brave to tackle the new subject. If it's too "monstrous," we'll pull the covers over our head and deny its existence.

Most of us have been confronted with at least one "monster" in our lifetime. Some of them have been difficult or even traumatic. Here's a look at some "monsters" you might recognize, and how we dealt with them.

When I was five years old, I was sure that a real, live you-can-touch-him Santa Claus existed. Mom and Dad—and my older brother—had told me so. On every Christmas Eve, we put up the tree in the living room and decorated it. We set out the tray with milk and cookies.

On every Christmas morning, the cookies and milk were gone, footprints of ash led from the fireplace to the tree and back, and presents sat piled up. Santa Claus must have stuffed himself down our very own chimney in Long Island, New York, on Christmas Eve during the night while I was sleeping.

But on this Christmas Eve, my brother threw Santa under the bus. (You probably know the "throwing under the bus" metaphor for turning against someone.) "Santa Claus doesn't exist," he said. "It's all Mom and Dad's doing."

"Noooo!" I didn't believe this outright lie. But he was my brother, and I looked up to him, so maybe he could be telling the truth. He'd always told the truth before, and my parents did, too—or so I had thought until then.

The idea that Santa didn't exist was monstrous! Suddenly, two distinct, opposite possibilities confronted me—Santa did or Santa did not exist.

The idea that Santa did *not* exist was a "monster."

I was determined to find out—to see Santa in real life. So, after dinner, I sat on the stairs, leaning against the banister, determined to stay up and see Santa heave his hefty belly out of the fireplace with a fat red sack of presents.

Alas, I fell asleep.

I awoke in the morning to see the presents under the tree, ash footprints on the carpet, and no cookies or milk left. Santa had come!

But my trusted brother had planted the seed of doubt. I began to think about the thousands of families all over the world who expected Santa to arrive, the many homes without chimneys, and whether reindeer really flew. My older brother had cut a chink in my five-and-a-half-year-old armor of accepting truth from adults. I was experiencing two competing thoughts simultaneously. How would I deal with them?

Here are some other "monsters" you might have experienced yourself, or witnessed in someone else you have known.

The parents of a young white girl told her that Black people were inferior or dangerous. When she saw Black people as she grew up, she felt a vague fear—they were so different from her, and they were usually portrayed as criminals or rioters on her family's cable TV news station. Black people seemed to be "monsters."

To a young Black boy, the police seemed to be "monsters," constantly arresting teens in his neighborhood and jailing them for minor offenses, or maybe nothing. Cops seemed as if they were "monsters."

Growing up in a Christian church where the pastor said, "Every word of the Bible is literally true," a young woman believed the messages in Genesis that God created the earth and everything in it in seven human-calendar days, and that men have one less rib than women because God pulled a rib from Adam to make Eve. When taught in science class that men and women have the same number of ribs, and that the earth evolved over the course of several million years, she was confronted with a "monster." Was God, as she learned about Him through her pastor and her Bible, absolutely right? Or was science right? The two stories seemed completely incompatible.

In 1972, members of then-President Nixon's re-election campaign broke into and burglarized the Democratic headquarters in the Watergate part of Washington, D.C. When the police caught the thieves, it quickly became clear that President Richard Nixon had lied about his involvement—he had taped every conversation he ever had. When you hear someone planning an event and then hear them deny it, you should be able to admit that they are telling a lie, and the burglary was also a crime.

My parents had been loyal Republicans their whole voting lives. They had supported Nixon, the candidate. They had voted for him. They believed in the fundamental Republican principles of limited government and caution in spending. They were both basically honest and conscientious people.

When my father saw Nixon's lies exposed on television, he said, "Nixon betrayed us."

But my mother said, "Nixon is an honest man."

Cognitive Dissonance and Confirmation Bias

Enter "cognitive dissonance"—also known as a "monster."

Cognitive dissonance is a mental state in which we—often unknowingly—hold two fundamentally conflicting ideas in our mind at the same time. We are confronted by a situation in which the information we have had up to this point comes into conflict with some new information.[6]

This definition may seem like gobbledygook to you. But if we get a handle on it, we'll all understand the voting and election crises (of 2020 and 2022) much better.

Another term for us to learn is "confirmation bias." That's when you interpret new evidence and observations to confirm and fit into pre-existing beliefs you already possess—whether valid or not.[7]

Back to Santa Claus. The cookies are gone, the presents have arrived, and Santa *does* exist.

My five-year-old mind was experiencing cognitive dissonance—that point when the mind is experiencing two conflicting ideas or emotions at the same time. The ideas are opposite. Both can't be true. Is there, or is there not, a Santa Claus?

I was also participating in "confirmation bias." All the facts lined up with my pre-existing beliefs, which Mom and Dad had fed me, and even—up until then—my brother. The milk, the cookies, the ashen footprints, and all the presents—Santa had to be real! I had crammed all the information I *wanted* to believe into my old belief. Whatever my brother said was a lie, a fabrication. I could cram his allegations about Santa into my beliefs, too. Nothing had to change, because my brother was lying!

But we have been given minds as well as emotions. We can feel and we can think. By my sixth birthday, with the gentle acknowledgement of my parents, and my brilliant analytical six-year-old mind, I figured out that: 1) Santa couldn't get to every house that needed him on Christmas Eve; 2) not all houses had chimneys; and 3) reindeer don't fly. More concrete evidence existed than my five-year-old mind had considered. My parents had also created a safe space in which they encouraged me to learn new things. I began to realize that there was more information about Santa Claus than I had previously been aware of.

So, I gave up my old idea and adopted a new one—the *Spirit* of Santa Claus is very much alive. Hanukkah, the lamp that miraculously burned for eight days in the temple, and Christmas, the miraculous gift of the Christ Child, stir in us the spirit of love and generosity. I moved from the childish belief in a fat, jolly, red-suited man at the North Pole to Santa as a metaphor for miracles, love, and generosity.

A metaphor is when we say that something which *resembles* another *is* another. It's a figure of speech comparing two unlike things that have something in common, but without using the word "like" or "as."[8]

For example, the world *is* a stage. John *is* a night owl. My brother threw Santa under the bus. And, finally, there is an article from the editor of a newspaper years ago, saying, "Yes, Virginia, there is a Santa Claus."

We know that the world is not the same as a stage, yet we can imagine people "getting on stage" and acting their part. We know that John is not an owl, but he does stay up late at night as owls do (and sleeps late in the morning).

We also know that there wasn't a bus, and my brother did not throw Santa under it. What did happen was that my brother "outed" Santa as not a real person when I believed the lovely myth that Santa came down our chimney and ate our cookies.

So, when it comes to Santa Claus, do we worry as adults if Santa is literally an immortal jolly human who lives at the North Pole surrounded by elves, ready to harness his flying reindeer to the chariot on Christmas Eve and deliver presents to millions of good children?

No. Santa is a metaphor for the spirit of love, generosity, and giving to others. Looking back, the editor of that newspaper did Virginia no favors. He insisted that there was a Santa Claus and that her "little" friends were all wrong. A better editor might have explained the metaphor to Virginia. She was already eight years old.[9]

For little children whose minds are not yet fully developed, a literal Santa Claus makes sense. But as we mature (into the first or second grade), we begin to understand symbols and metaphors.

It's okay not to be literal. It is more than okay; it is often the right thing to do. It's important to know the difference between the literal—a feeling of generosity—and the metaphorical—jolly ol' Santa.

In one of the Hebrew psalms, David says, "The Lord is my rock, my fortress, and my deliverer."

We know that the Lord is not a literal rock or a fortress. As humans, we understand these physical things. In the Psalm, the poet uses the metaphors "rock" and "fortress" to convey the strength of his faith in the Lord.

Similarly, Jesus has said, "Ye are the Salt of the Earth," and "Do not hide your light under a bushel basket."

We know humans are not cubes of salt. However, we can understand Jesus' metaphor as he admonished us to provide enrichment to the world, just as salt enriches the flavor of our food. Most of us do not carry around an oil lamp and would not even recognize a bushel basket. Nevertheless, we innately understand the metaphor about showing our better spiritual qualities to the world.

Likewise, in the book of Genesis, we Jews, Christians, and Muslims have all been taught that God created the world in seven days. Some people insist that the Earth actually came into existence in seven human-timed days about 5,000 years ago. The creation story from scientists can appear to be a "monster."

The scientific, factual evidence of various phenomena—rocks, mountains, canyons, oceans, and the fossils of numerous creatures—indicates an earthly existence spanning hundreds of millions of years as understood in human terms. And, as noted, if you ever wind up dissecting a human body in medical school, you'll find that "Adam" has the same number of ribs as does "Eve."

"Seven days" makes much more sense as a metaphor. What is a human-designed "day," "night," or "week" to the Creator of the Universe? We can only use human concepts in our attempt to understand the unknown. So, perfectly devout religious people can hold the beautiful creation story in our hearts as true, in a profound sense, while also understanding that the authors of Genesis used mere human language—a metaphor—to explain the unknown.

Cognitive dissonance challenges our minds when both the *metaphorical* (perhaps taught as literal) and the *scientific* clash as we learn of the existence of two apparently incompatible ideas. Sometimes the anxiety over the conflict is too big to manage. What we worry about becomes a "monster."

Confirmation bias is our tendency to interpret new information in a way that supports an existing belief. For example, I have a friend who believes in election fraud. When I told him that our county elections were a hundred percent fraud-proof, he said, "Well, I bet there's plenty of fraud in other states." He wanted to maintain his belief in fraudulent elections by insisting there's fraud somewhere.

Cognitive dissonance may be a significant factor in the challenges we have faced in trying to understand the 2020 elections. Several big ideas may have been monsters for us in 2020 without our even realizing it: 1) all the laws around the elections; 2) the voting machinery and process; 3) the surprise attack by COVID-19; and 4) the lies, disinformation, and conspiracy theories spread by then-President Donald Trump and his allies.

CHAPTER 8

THE MONSTER OF ELECTION LAWS

We take an oath or affirmation to uphold the Constitution—our U.S. Constitution, and our State Constitution. We're a nation of laws. No one is supposed to be above the law. We're law-abiding citizens. We believe in law and order. Those who break the law should be held accountable and brought to justice.

Yeah. It's actually a lot to take in. It can be overwhelming for non-lawyers (most Americans) to try to understand the complexities of it all. Similar to a cognitively dissonant monster, it's TMI—too much information. Worse yet, the people telling the truth about election law—the good guys—are the ones handing you a "monster."

To break it down, here are the major laws that affect how we vote. Try not to let your eyes glaze over. I put toothpicks in my eyelids (metaphorically) to keep them open.

1. Article 1, Section 4, in the United States Constitution refers to the times, places, and manner of holding elections for Senators and Representatives (of Congress). This clause is brief, vague, and provides Congress with the opportunity to enact additional laws on the subject.[10]

2. Amendment 12 to the Constitution, ratified in 1804, revised the outlines and procedure on how Presidents and Vice-Presidents of the U.S. were to be elected. This Amendment is lengthy and verbose, and open to more than one interpretation.

3. In Arizona, we have a constitution—a mere 108 pages—with a long and strong Declaration of Rights. Among other things, "all political power is inherent in the people, and governments derive their just powers from the consent of the governed, and are established to protect and maintain individual rights."[11]

4. The Arizona Revised Statutes (A.R.S.) flesh out the Arizona Constitution. A.R.S. § 16 governs elections in Arizona. Even the *outline* of chapters is about ten pages long.

5. Supplementing the Arizona Constitution and A.R.S. § 16 is the Arizona Secretary of State's *Elections Procedures Manual (EPM or Manual)*. It is almost 300 pages long. Typically, the Secretary of State will submit their proposed *EPM* to the Governor every other year, by October 1 of each odd-numbered year. The Governor must approve the *EPM* by December 31.

The *EPM* ensures statewide consistency, legality, and efficiency in election administration throughout the state. Individual counties may, in addition, have their own procedures; however, these procedures cannot conflict with the *EPM,* as it has the force of law.

This information is all far too much for me, and probably for you—unless you are an elections worker.

Here are samples of laws or *EPM* guidelines—a mere sampling that no one reads for fun. Keep those toothpicks in place!

1. Just approving the *Manual* is a project. The County Recorder may suggest updates to the Secretary of State (SOS) about the *Manual* every election year. These are the rules they think they must and will

follow. But the final word is with the SOS and the Governor.

2. Voters may request an early ballot to send in by mail. They must show an Arizona Driver's License or an Arizona non-operating ID card issued by the Motor Vehicle Division.

3. Every requirement in the *Manual* is referenced to an Arizona Statute. For example, if someone does not have a permanent home or address and wants to register to vote, they may complete the "No Residence Address Confirmation" Form, as provided in the *Manual,* which they must sign and date.[12]

4. A lot goes into ensuring that the actual polling places are fair, that no one will harass you, and that your vote is private. There can be observers, but they may not wear, carry, or display any materials that identify or express support for or opposition to a political party, organization, candidate, or ballot measure.[13]

5. Observers may take handwritten notes during observation, but they must use a writing instrument of a color designated by the officer in charge of the election or procedure. Currently, it's red.

6. Political party representatives may observe at a central counting place and at each point where ballots are handled or transferred from one election official to another.

7. The County Board of Supervisors must canvass (examine with scrutiny) the official election results in a public meeting by the required deadline...
For primary elections and Presidential Preference Elections [PPEs]...within 10 business days after the election;[14]

8. For …general elections…, between six and 20 days after the election.[15]
9. On top of that, the Arizona Secretary of State must canvass the results for any elections that include a federal, statewide, or legislative office…for primary elections and PPEs, on or before the third Monday after the election.[16]

Phew!

There are hundreds of categories in which election workers must follow the directions of the *Manual*. A sample includes:

> Voter Registration forms, Voter Registration requirements, Voter Registration Assistance Agencies, Voter Registration Deadlines, Early Voting—Ballot by Mail and Early On-Site voting, Challenges to Early Ballots, Ballot-by-Mail Elections, Voting Equipment, Accommodating Voters with Disabilities, Presidential Preference Election, Appointment and Training of Poll Workers and other Election Staff, Election Day Operations, Central Counting Place Procedures, Hand Count Audit, Post-Election Day Procedures, Certifying Election Results, and, when required, Conducting an Automatic Recount.

There's more.

If your eyes and mind glazed over, you're not alone. Trying to understand all this stuff is similar to confronting a "monster." The actual business of voting is complicated, and the laws governing it are long, complex, and subject to change.

There are two points for us to keep in mind here.

First, voting law is complex, and because we are a nation where no one is supposed to be above the law, there are laws to govern each aspect of the process. It applies to everyone and all elections.

Second, when faced with such a "monster"—that's right—the mental monster of what voting actually involves, it's easy to see why some of us let ourselves believe false accusations of election fraud. I can't understand all the voting laws. You can't either. Someone alleged fraud. Maybe there is fraud. With so much going on, there must be....

Why not take a shortcut?

We shouldn't.

We must acknowledge the risks associated with election officials not abiding by election rules and procedures. We need to put our trust in the hundreds, actually thousands, and maybe millions of Americans who participate in making our elections work fairly, efficiently, and according to law.

If we refuse to accept the laws and if we don't trust the integrity of election workers, we've allowed the un-Constitutional, illegal monster—the big LIE—to take over. When we seek an easy fix that is outside the laws that we, the people, have established, we revert to the rule before our 1776 Revolution—rule by a lawless King or tyrant. We may think he is on our side this time, but we are all expendable. He'll throw us under the bus whenever it's convenient.

If you're a legal nerd (and we need you), go ahead and read all the laws and the *Manual.* Even though I practiced law for many years, I still don't want to know it all.

What I can say is that, because of the number of players in the elections arena—from thousands of poll workers of all major political parties (and independents) to County Recorder and the Board of Supervisors to the Attorney General, I feel safe trusting them to do the work to make the voting system the best possible. At the very least, most are competent. Better yet, they don't all agree. That's how and why they'll keep each other from cheating.

52

CHAPTER 9

THE MONSTERS OF COVID-19 AND RACE

On January 21, 2020, while a friend and I walked down the street in Edmonds, Washington, a town north of Seattle, we saw two Chinese-American girls wearing masks. "How silly, how paranoid," we Yankees thought. At that point, only one case of COVID-19 had been detected—in that very town. *We* weren't going to need masks.

It was election season, with elections scheduled for March, August, and November.

By mid-March, the COVID-19 story had dramatically changed. On March 20, 2020, the AZ Department of Health Services reported the first COVID death in Arizona. By May 15, there were 13,169 recorded cases and 651 deaths. By June 8, there were 27,678 cases of COVID-19 in Arizona and 1,047 reported deaths.[17]

COVID-19 hit us by storm. As a pretty healthy nation, we weren't used to pandemics or ravaging diseases as the norm. Following the significant scare of Polio in the 1940s and 1950s, Dr. Jonas Salk developed a vaccine to counter the virus. Millions of Americans rushed to get their shots, and in a few years, Polio almost disappeared in the U.S. as a disease.

But we also had the backdrop of hundreds of thousands of Americans doubting science. Ever since the 1920s and the Scopes trial on whether a teacher could teach evolution of plants and animals in the classroom as a scientific "truth," many people from evangelical and literalist traditions have come to believe that science and scientific enquiry do not provide valid, truthful evidence of the creation of the world. Only Genesis did. God created the world in seven days—seven human days—not the millions of years evidenced by scientific study.

A large group of Americans were primed to reject science if it conflicted with what they had learned in church about the truth.[18]

As soon as COVID-19 arrived, we, as a nation, ran into trouble. Some pastors and self-proclaimed doctors said COVID-19 was not a real viral epidemic and that a vaccine would not prevent us from getting the disease.

Meanwhile, the evidence coming from the Centers for Disease Control (CDC) changed, and their recommendations changed. Did they know what they were doing?

Finally, the President of the United States, Donald Trump, minimized the problem and continued to make inaccurate, fake pronouncements. Why? Who knows? But, for example, he said in January 2020, "We have it totally under control. It's one person coming in from China. It's going to be just fine." In February, he said, "It miraculously goes away," and "The fifteen cases in the U.S. within a couple of days are going to be down close to zero."

In March, as doctors, members of Congress, and Dr. Fauci of the Centers for Disease Control sounded the alarm, Mr. Trump said, "It'll go away."[19]

In the spring of 2020, it became clear to all public health officials that COVID-19 was not going away. It became an enormous threat to the health of millions of us in the U.S. When officials began to talk of mandatory mask-wearing in public buildings, social distancing, closing businesses, restaurants, and schools, some political and religious leaders pooh-poohed the virus and clamored for our religious freedom to choose—or not to choose—vaccines. The President publicly insulted and criticized Dr. Fauci, the head of the CDC, and a science-based public health medical professional for his entire adult life. Our country was in a public health and political crisis.

As if that wasn't enough, on May 26, 2020, the nation watched as a video went viral of the knee-on-his-throat killing of a Black man, George Floyd, by a white cop. The facts were pretty straightforward. The police officer whose knee was on Floyd's throat for over nine minutes did not change his position, even while Floyd pleaded, "I can't breathe." Then Floyd died.

They had stopped Floyd on suspicion of perhaps using a counterfeit $20 bill at a convenience store—a nonviolent offense of which he had not even been charged, much less tried and proven guilty. Suddenly, he was dead.

A huge, angry eruption, shaping into "Black Lives Matter," swept this nation and the world. Demonstrations occurred in many major cities. Ultimately, numerous protests broke out at night, and some individuals destroyed property.

Meanwhile, the footage on Officer Derek Chauvin was clear, with a recording of him kneeling on Floyd's neck for 9 minutes and 29 seconds. He did nothing, and three other officers nearby did not urge him to make any change. All four were arrested. Their trials coincided with the COVID-19 pandemic ravaging the nation and the upcoming Primaries and General Election.

Ultimately, police officer Chauvin was convicted of second-degree murder. In June 2021, he was sentenced to twenty-two-and-a-half years in prison.[20]

If it didn't occur to us at the time that COVID-19 and the Floyd murder/trial/protests/Black Lives Matter movement were too much to absorb—that they were both "monsters"—perhaps now we can see how, for many of us, they were.[21]

People conditioned to think of Blacks as scary or potentially criminal can more easily believe that what happened was large, damaging riots. People conditioned to think that White police are violent or criminal can more easily believe that the police caused the violence. To some extent, we are all viewing these events through the lens of our own cultural "monsters."

COVID-19 was caught in the crosshairs between scientists and faith-based beliefs that opposed scientific evidence, particularly when it conflicted with specific words in the Bible, and a President who lacked both scientific understanding and religious faith.

Race became a factor because it is almost always a factor in American life and politics. Many whites, who grew up without close positive experiences with Blacks, saw the riots as a threat to law and order. Many Blacks, who had grown up with negative experiences of racial discrimination and bad experiences with police, saw Floyd's killing as part of an ongoing violation of law and order by law enforcement officers.

Overwhelmed by election laws, the pandemic of COVID-19, and with a permanent backdrop of racial tension, many Americans moved through the 2020 election season with more uncertainty and distrust in at least one government entity than we had experienced in many decades.

We may not have known it at the time, but we were vulnerable to fear, lies, and manipulation.

CHAPTER 10

THE MONSTER OF ELECTION LIES

The COVID-19 pandemic monster was only one area in which lies and mis/disinformation assaulted our trust. Racial division was yet another. Third, political lies posed an even greater threat to our democracy and trust in the electoral system.

We've seen numerous politicians lie before. Two standouts in my memory are President Bill Clinton alleging, "I did not have sex with that woman," and President George W. Bush, after the disastrous Katrina hurricane in New Orleans, praising his FEMA Director, Michael D. Brown, "Brownie's doing a heck of a job."

We've become somewhat immune to the impact of political lies and misrepresentations.

But we should be aware.

In 2016, Hillary Clinton won the Democratic nomination for President after Barack Obama served two terms. Trump, who won the Republican nomination, started early on saying that the elections were probably "rigged" (Trump's words) in favor of Clinton.[22] He repeatedly insulted his opponent, referring to her as "Crooked Hillary." Since there had been some issues in Arkansas in her past, and some emails as Secretary of State, it was mentally easy for some who favored Trump, or the general Republican philosophy, to slip into a belief that indeed, Ms. Clinton was "crooked." But in the realm of political conduct, she was not.

Then came the election. The truth was that Hillary Clinton won the popular vote by almost three million votes.

However, due to a strong showing in several significant states, Trump secured enough electoral votes to win the presidency through the Electoral College system. Suddenly, all that talk about the election being "rigged" disappeared. For Trump, an election was only "rigged" if he lost.

There was widespread dissatisfaction with the Trump Presidency from 2017 to 2020. Former Vice President Joe Biden won the Democratic nomination for the 2020 race. Sensing that he might not win, Mr. Trump again made numerous false or misleading statements about the elections during the entire campaign, including:

- Mischaracterizations and false accusations about the voting and counting process;
- False claims about barred observers and lack of verification;
- Baseless examples of supposed fraud;
- Conspiracy theories about voting machines; and
- Comments suggesting but not proving fraud.

On dozens of occasions, Mr. Trump characterized the election as "rigged," "stolen," or "a hoax."[23]

Why is there more to say about his continued lying, misinformation, and conspiracy theories about voting? Because with Donald J. Trump (as of 2025, in his second presidency) and his allies, the lies have grown out of control and become more destructive. These lies threaten our democratic institutions and way of life.

Let's think about lying and its impact. Most of us learned as children that it is imperative to tell the truth. Yet, virtually all of us lie at some point. Lying often hurts someone while benefiting another.

When I was little, my brother lied to my parents, telling them I had stolen the cookie. My dad spanked me. My brother was not punished. Lying worked to his benefit, even though it was wrong.

When might we be willing to lie? Here are some lies:

- Hitler (in Germany) blaming the Jews (and other minorities) as a pretense and justification for genocide and imperialism.

- Rationalizing by lying to yourself: "I'm a good person, so I'm not doing something bad."
- Going along with your friends' lies about someone so you won't be an outsider.

There are many ways to lie. As we mature, we realize that lying is wrong and telling the truth is right, even when we fear negative consequences as a result.

Anyone can lie or make false accusations. Coming from the President of the United States, the repetition of such lies and falsehoods has unsettled the people of our country more than ever.

Let's move on. We'll take a deep dive into how elections work, what occurred during election season in 2020, how six men stopped the steal of the election, and the aftermath. Finally, we'll consider what our future might hold. First, voting and elections.

PART THREE

UNDERSTANDING THE VOTE

"Voting impacts every area of our lives, from health care to jobs to racial justice. When we vote, we're choosing the people and the laws that shape the direction of our communities. Using our power and voting makes sure we have voice in the future."

—League of Women Voters of California Education Fund

CHAPTER 11

WHY WE VOTE

By the time you read this book, you will have studied the Boston Tea Party in school. It happened over 250 years ago, but it remains a part of our history and is a fundamental tenet of our American principles.

The colonies along the East Coast of the United States were a part of the British Empire. The King imposed taxes on goods entering the colonies for his own benefit, not for the benefit of the colonies. The colonies had no power to disagree. So, a bunch of rowdies—patriots for the colonies—boarded the British boats in Boston Harbor and threw all the tea into the ocean rather than paying taxes on the tea.

This act of rebellion mushroomed into a movement: "no taxation without representation," meaning no taxation *without the right to vote*. One of our fundamental tenets, as the Founding Fathers of the USA assembled a constitution and laws, was that we should have the right to vote if we are required to pay taxes. We should have a say in how the government spends our money.

Well, not everyone. Women, slaves, and men without property couldn't vote. Those rights would come later with improvements and changes to our laws and Constitution. One of the first and fundamental values of our nation is the right to vote.

Ever since the beginning, there has also been resistance to the right of some people to vote. Men opposed the right of women to vote. Whites tried to prevent Blacks from voting. Our laws now almost uniformly allow voting only upon becoming eighteen years of age. Most states prohibit non-citizens and convicted felons—and dead people—from voting. You can vote only once. As you can imagine, there's a lot to squabble about.

When I began to examine the vote in Maricopa County in 2020—only one county in the entire United States—I felt overwhelmed. It was too big, too complex, with too many machines, too many people, too many officials, and too many processes, checks, inspections, inspectors, and challenges.

The 2020 elections—just in Maricopa County—were, to me, a MONSTER!

So, I gave myself the "talk." I'm a grownup. I've lived a relatively long time, and I have learned a lot—elementary school grammar and math, high school French and physics, and how to take a train by myself to an unfamiliar city. Some of what we learn comes from experience, while some comes from education, training, and specialized expertise. No one has it all. I could coach under-8 soccer even today, but I wouldn't know a thing about chess, or—more to our book's point—voting machines.

I decided to break it down into what seemed to be logical elements:

Ch. 12. Machines, locations, and physical stuff;
Ch. 13. People and agencies responsible for doing the job;
Ch. 14. Processes set up before, during, and after; and
Ch. 15. Security.

Let's start with the physical stuff—machines, paper ballots, locations, and Sharpies and other writing devices.

CHAPTER 12

MACHINES AND MORE

We may have a sense of how complicated voting is by examining the laws, without even reading them. The entire organizing effort aimed at getting a vote cast deserves a special, focused look. I'm willing myself to be brave and learn something vast and new by reaching beyond my "monster"—my desire to reject this huge new subject. It has become a safe learning space for me.

How do you feel? Have you felt daunted by the significant topic of the voting process? Have you believed conspiracy theories about fraud and malfunctions? I hope you'll be brave and willing to consider this new information rather than allow fear to block a potential change in your own understanding. The details of this topic are a lot to take in.

We've organized the information in the chronological sequence of events. We may combine various elements, including machines and locations, within a single chapter. Do your best.

Before the Vote

Let's start with the ballots.

1. First, we need a printer to make ballots. That is pretty easy to do—most commercial printers will work. Check.

2. Second, we need the proper paper for ballots. The required paper stock will not bleed through to the other side when you use a black pen, markers, or "Sharpies," as might be provided. That's not hard

to do. Paper can be manufactured in a variety of thicknesses—think about the thickness of the pages in a book versus a poster, and then consider cardboard boxes. Check.

3. Third, there's the size of the ballot page. Again, not that hard to do. Think about postcards, letters, posters. One-sided or two-sided. Again, we're familiar with page sizes. Check.

Meanwhile, they sometimes need to have different "styles." Most ballots have a lot of those ovals we fill in. For folks with braille needs, there is another "style." The different cities may have different measures on their ballot, leading to more styles. So, as part of the ballot requirements, check.

However, during the COVID-19 pandemic, some doubted whether the County could find the right kind of paper for a complete supply for each of the three elections scheduled for 2020—the Presidential Preference Election in March, the Primaries in August, and the General Election in November. Check, with worry and extra effort.

Then, during the 2022 elections, issues arose with 80 vs. 100 lb. paper and 19" vs. 20" ballots. Let it go for now.

Getting all of this right is a human's job. Later.

4. Fourth, we need to know that the people who vote are eligible (18 years old or more, citizens, alive) to vote. Computers and programs receive and store all this information for every registered individual in the state, updating it as necessary throughout the year and maintaining voter privacy. This task requires special computers with a hard drive and a program. It can be done—just not by me. Consider it done with expertise and diligence. Check.

During the Voting Season

Some of this information is a repetition of the previous section, but we need to understand when they use specific items and for what purpose. Here goes:

5. Fifth, we need machines into which we insert our ballots—that record every oval, candidate, and ballot measure. Meanwhile, we need a different machine to record the fact that I came here and voted. That machine will tell every other similar machine in the County that I voted—only once. If I try to sneak into another polling place to vote again, or bring my dead mother's ballot, it will have records of her death as well. Dead people can't vote—ask computers in the offices of the County Recorder, local newspapers, and the Department of Motor Vehicles. They coordinate information on deceased persons. Thanks, machines. Check.

6. Sixth, we need boxes or lockable bags into which all the ballots at all the voting centers go, which are secure so that no one can get in and tamper with them. Check.

7. Seventh, election officials drive to the central voting center with the ballots in a locked container. Screened staff put ballots with verifiable signatures into tabulation machines not connected to anything else. They have their own special, secure program. The best systems are researched and certified at a national level. Then, the County buys or leases them and gets them set up. They are called tabulation machines. Envelopes (with ballots inside)

with unverifiable signatures are sent to a different building for special scrutiny. Check.

8. Eighth, we need trucks or cars to transport the ballots from every polling place to "Grand Central," where the votes are tabulated. Ford? GM? Honda? I have no idea. But getting the trucks is easy. Check.

    Most of the machines and trucks are used on Election Day. However, there is a month of early voting available to people, with Vote Centers, Drop-Box-Only sites, and 24-Hour Ballot Drop Boxes, all of which are listed on the County website.

9. Ninth, the locations. The Vote Centers are buildings open for 28 days before Election Day. They could be a school, a church, a gymnasium—usually a rented space set up with in-person voting machines and booths, and staffed. They are monitored by bipartisan staff (when the sites are operating).

    The Drop-Box-Only sites are locations inside many city and town clerk's offices. While there is usually no in-person voting, staff do monitor the Drop Box sites.

    There are only two 24-Hour Ballot Drop Boxes—one outside the elections office in Phoenix, and one in Mesa. The Drop Box is bolted to the ground, available for ballot-dropping (inside your ID envelope) 24 hours a day, and monitored 24/7 by security cameras.

    All the Ballot Drop Boxes are visibly marked as official Drop Boxes, locked with a small opening for the envelope that the voter has signed before placing their ballot inside. Only specific Election Department officials have a key to open the box.

That's about it for machines and paper. Let's not forget the markers.

10. Tenth, at the polling locations, when they hand you an implement for filling out your ballot, they will probably give you a Sharpie. Why? Because, believe it or not, the ink on the Sharpie dries faster than any other ink, including the ballpoint. Therefore, it won't run or smudge when you put your ballot into the box or machine, wherever it goes next. Visit any office supply store, and you can buy a Sharpie. Check.

    If we fill out a mail-in ballot at home, we likely use our own pen—preferably black. We then fold it up and stick it in the envelope. That usually takes us a little time—time for the ink to dry.

11. Eleventh: Tamper-Evident Seals, Transport Bins, Serial Numbers, and Logs. When ballots are picked up, the sealed envelopes are placed in a transport bin secured by a tamper-evident seal. Each seal has a serial number logged into a transport statement, signed by ballot couriers and either the inspector or a designated government official.

You probably didn't notice the serial number or bar code on the outside of your mail-in envelope. It's like that. Numerous seals, codes, and computer-generated information that we often overlook make the ballots and their transport more secure.

Meanwhile, they allow poll watchers (people who attend to oversee the voting process at polling stations) to use red pens for writing other than voting at any of these centers. Why? Because the machines cannot register red. You can't use a red pen to cheat by marking up a ballot.

Even when we talk only about machines, Sharpies, and other physical stuff, we end up talking about people and things getting done, and ballots moving from one place to another.

We begin to realize—or remember—that there is more to the vote than one Election Day. At the very least, there is the request for and sending out of an early ballot. What about the locations that operate where you can vote or drop off your early ballot before Election Day? Who is in charge of that? On Election Day, many centers are open to receive voters, and, at the end of the day—literally—poll workers, politicians, and elected and appointed officials have to oversee the counting process. Many of these individuals stay through the night and into the next day to complete the job.

Who are all these people? What are they responsible for?

CHAPTER 13

WHO IS RESPONSIBLE?

Voting in an election in a county like Maricopa County involves many levels of responsibility.

National Responsibility

Nationally, the United States Election Assistance Commission (EAC) is an independent government agency (comprised of Republicans and Democrats). The EAC uses experts and tech nerds to test federal voting systems. The EAC also sets uniform national standards that all states and counties must meet when conducting elections.

This process of developing standards applies to elections for Congressional, Senate, and Presidential/Vice-Presidential candidates. It can include elections for other offices, such as state governor and county recorder, for example.

State Responsibility

The Arizona Legislature is responsible for enacting the laws about the Arizona election system. Every state will have its own laws that everyone within the state must follow.

The Secretary of State is responsible for preparing the *Election Procedures Manual (EPM),* which the Governor must approve every other year. Every county must follow the rules of the *EPM.*

Keep in mind the goal of our election system, which is to ensure that all eligible persons are registered and can vote safely and privately. We must respect the right that applies to us—and to the people who may vote differently from us.

In Maricopa County—as with all counties—the Arizona Secretary of State is responsible for performing a Logic and Accuracy (L&A) test on all voting equipment *prior to* each election. That includes "jurisdictional" elections (possibly at the city or school district level), County, State, and National elections. It consists of the Primary (within Parties), the Presidential Preference Election, and the General Election. More ahead on each.

County Responsibility

The Maricopa County Board of Supervisors (BOS) is responsible for overseeing in-person voting, Election Day voting, and tabulation.

The Elections Department (ED) has two co-directors. One reports directly to the BOS. The other reports directly to the County Recorder. The ED handles in-person voting on Election Day, emergency voting, and tabulation of all the ballots.

The Maricopa County Recorder's Office is responsible for handling early voting, maintaining voter files of active registered voters (over 2.6 million), processing early ballots, mail-in ballots, and overseeing drop-off sites and early voting centers.

As we can see, these responsibilities are enormous. There's a lot to do—on a good day.

The Maricopa County Sheriff's Office (MCSO) is also responsible for ensuring the safety of the polling places, the delivery of ballots to the ultimate voting center (the MCTEC), and the tabulation of ballots by election workers.

The Police Departments of each city may also be involved, including an in-house Election Information Security officer who works directly with Maricopa County's Office of Election Technology (MCTEC) and Arizona's Anti-Terrorism coordinating body (ACTIC).

Sometimes, the County, especially the MCSO, coordinates with national law enforcement agencies, such as the FBI and the Department of Homeland Security.[24]

As registered voters who cast our votes, we elect the Secretary of State, the County Recorder, the County Sheriff, and all five members of the Board of Supervisors. While these elected officials are usually not all from the same political party, they have a shared responsibility—to make the elections free, fair, safe, private, secure, and transparent. "Private" means no one will know how you voted. "Transparent" means that journalists, members of at least the two major political parties, and members of the public can observe or learn that the machinery is accurate to national standards, all the equipment and processes are proper, and that the election results are accurate.

Political Parties' Responsibility

For most elections, both Republican and Democratic representatives must, by custom and practice, be present together at polling places and centers where ballots are tabulated to ensure that one side does not cheat the other and that they agree on the results. For example, they sometimes verify the signature on an envelope against the one in the voting records to confirm its validity. When the machine fails to process a mail-in ballot, trained staff may need to call the voter to clarify their intended choice for a candidate or ballot measure.

Your Responsibility

And finally, you—the voting-eligible public individual—have the responsibility to get yourself registered, keep up with your status, make a one-time request for a mail-in ballot, find your nearest Vote Center, and get answers to all your questions. It's your job to vote according to the law and to behave in a way that ensures the safety of all others.

CHAPTER 14

THE VOTING PROCESS

A. Before the Vote

For an election to proceed smoothly, everything must be in place, which includes having the necessary locations to vote, all the required equipment, and all the staff, volunteers, and other personnel needed to run all parts of the election system. Most election workers throughout Maricopa County and the United States are honest citizens, similar to you and me, who want the elections to be free, fair, open to all eligible voters, and private.

The process must also be transparent so that the general public can see and agree that it was fair.

1. First, the Arizona Legislature has passed numerous laws relating to elections over many decades with periodic changes, improvements, and updates, generally intended to ensure a fair election process.

2. Second, the Secretary of State creates an *Elections Procedures Manual (EPM)* in compliance with Arizona Law, which s/he submits to both the Governor of Arizona and the Attorney General. Both of those officials must sign off on the *EPM* as the accepted guideline for the upcoming election. Every election official in every county must follow the guidelines in the *EPM*, which means they must be familiar with its contents and agree to abide by them. The *EPM* has the effect of law.

Be aware that some individuals do not wish to play by the rules. They may be candidates, elected officials, or overzealous volunteers. That's partly why the system has so many checks and security features. To make sure everyone plays by the rules.

3. Third, regarding the machinery and the computer programs, we'll start with the hash code. It is a unique code composed of a series of numbers and/or letters assigned to each file and program for the versions of software and applications installed on the certified Election Management System (EMS).

   The EMS consists of tabulation equipment, servers, desktop computers, central count tabulators, vote center tabulators, and adjudication stations.

   After the suite of files and programs obtains federal certification, the certified Voting System Testing Laboratory (VSTL) generates a series of unique hash codes using a hash code generator. The hash code generator evaluates each line of data, text or code within each file of the various versions of installed software.

   After the hash code generator has completed its evaluations, it assigns the hash codes to that trusted build that is certified for use by the U.S. Elections Assistance Commission. (This is over my head, since I don't have computer training.)

   Before every election, the Tabulation Team, supervised by the Elections Department (ED), performs a hash code verification test. This test compares the hash codes of the installed files on the tabulation equipment with the certified hash codes provided to the ED by the U.S. Elections Assistance Commission.

After performing the test, the ED notifies the Secretary of State (SOS) of the completed test and must confirm that the two hash code tests matched. The ED then provides the SOS with a copy of the Election Program that the ED will use in the upcoming election. The Election Program contains the program files that passed the hash code verification test.

4. Fourth, the Elections Department performs a series of logic and accuracy tests. They perform an L&A test of all (one hundred percent) of the equipment and contests (i.e., federal, state, legislative, county, local). The test takes a few weeks to complete before the SOS's L&A test. (Still beyond me.)

5. Fifth, the SOS performs a test of randomly selected equipment on election contests for which they are the filing official (i.e., federal, state, and legislative) before the upcoming election.

6. Sixth, after the SOS test, the ED performs another L&A test that is live-streamed and open to the public to attend. It is similar to the SOS test as it includes a random sampling of equipment, but the ED includes all contests on the ballot.

7. Seventh, when the ED makes its second L&A test, the SOS is in the room, and the ED generates a copy of the results and gives them to the SOS after the test is complete, verified and signed off by the representatives of the two major political parties.

By the way, no one can make a change to a file without being detected. Here's an example: you write a letter (Word document) on your PC. Someone could use the hash code generator to evaluate that letter. It would evaluate each character, including capitalization, font types, bolding, headers, footers, and spaces. If you go back in and change that letter in any way, even one comma, the hash code verification tool would identify that change and your letter (document) would not pass the test!

All of this information is over my head—like a "monster"—because it is too much for me to grasp. I'm not a computer nerd. Sometimes I'd rather pick the easy way of thinking—we only have paper ballots, and someone is conspiring to stuff the ballot box.

However, my simple fear-fantasy is not what happens. Nowadays, the use of computers and programs, and trained human experts, drives the accuracy of the voting system. I trust that the individuals in charge—computer experts and from diverse political parties—know what they are doing. If I don't trust that part of it, I'll be susceptible to claims of a conspiracy to rig the election.

So, in summary, before each election (the Presidential Preference, followed by the Primary, and then the General), the machines and programs are verified by the ED and the SOS to confirm that the software system used for the election is the same system that underwent certification.

B. The Actual Vote

To request a mail-in ballot—a month before Election Day, a time specified in the *EPM*—we contact the office of the County Recorder that is set up by our government and taxpayer funds. They have computers, hired staff, and supplies to send mail-in ballots to all who request them. It is part of Arizona law—to send mail-in ballots to all those who request them—and *only* to those voters. Check.

The Arizona mail-in ballots come inside a large yellow envelope, along with a green, postage-free, coded mail-back envelope. Easy enough to produce? Sure. Check.

If you go to a voting location (a polling place or voting center), you will stand at a three-sided booth with the black Sharpie they've provided, and mark those ovals on your ballot. Not too difficult. Check.

However, during the COVID-19 pandemic, many schools, churches, and smaller voting centers abruptly canceled events due to fears of spreading the disease. County officials were responsible for renting alternate locations. Meanwhile, many poll workers cancelled due to illness or fear of contracting COVID-19. County officials in 2020 worked overtime to replace them.

We may receive our early-vote mail-in ballot through the mail. We can fill out that ballot at home and then mail it back or drop it off at any Vote Center or Drop Box Site.

Then, when we've completed our vote, we—or the volunteers or staff at any site, while we watch—put our ballot in a secure box. These boxes need to be constructed in such a way that the people at the polling center cannot open, stuff, or steal any ballots. Producing such boxes and ensuring they reach every voting center safely is something I understand (but wouldn't be able to do). Check.

Meanwhile, the ballots from the Vote Centers and Drop Box sites need to be transported to the Maricopa County Tabulation and Election Center (MCTEC). Two ballot couriers of differing parties pick up the signed and sealed early ballot packets every day that the location is open. All forms are reviewed and audited nightly when the transport bins are inspected at the MCTEC. The sealed envelopes are removed for early ballot processing.

C. Tabulating (Counting) the Vote

Finally, there are tabulation machines, specifically designed, manufactured, and pre- and post-checked for accuracy. Their job is to count every ballot and every vote for every candidate and every other measure on the ballot accurately, one hundred percent.

The electoral secure boxes are safely delivered to the big central building of the MCTEC, located in a different area from both the Office of the Maricopa County Recorder and the Maricopa County Board of Supervisors. Check.

The MCTEC has several unique features. Access to the building is restricted to those with a job responsibility or direct oversight of the tabulation process. Alternatively, during the non-election season, a group can arrange a tour on specific days. All visitors must be pre-approved and are escorted only to particular locations (most, but not all, rooms are available), and a staff member accompanies them at all times. During tabulation times, representatives and observers from political parties are always present, providing oversight. As noted for workers and observers at the polling stations, only red pens are allowed in the Ballot Tabulation Center, since the equipment cannot read red ink. No messing with ballots.

The tabulation machines do not have an internet connection or any external connection. The wiring is all visible—we've seen it— showing how tabulation equipment is routed directly to a secure server behind glass and on display for public view. It is accessible only to four authorized officials, with 24/7 video monitoring of the entire system.

It takes considerable skill and maintenance to make an election run successfully. Check, check, check.

D. After the Vote: Checking to Make Sure It Worked

Specialized audit machines ensure that all tabulation machines function correctly. The Secretary of State's trained staff conduct another Logic and Accuracy test.

If it is a close vote (i.e., the percentage specified by current law is less than 0.5%), an automatic recount will proceed. For the most part, the laws restrict hand counts to specific conditions.

The sources for this information include materials produced by MCTEC, the websites of the Arizona Secretary of State and Maricopa County, Arizona, statutes, the *Election Procedures Manual,* and emails from Supervisor Bill Gates and Scott Jarrett, co-director of the Election Department. We have attempted to provide thorough, accurate, and precise information. Some details may change, such as the legislative-mandated percentage that triggers a recount.

The entire voting process takes skill, training, and expertise to produce. It is way beyond my ability. Could you do it? As checks in the whole system (of people and machines) become more sophisticated and advanced, we need to trust that those with advanced training will perform their jobs properly.

CHAPTER 15

SECURITY

Most of what we're dealing with in this book is the elections in Maricopa County. That means that most of the responsibility for security falls in the hands of the Maricopa County Sheriff's Office (MCSO).

First, we need security personnel—Sheriff's Deputies—at the location where the votes are counted. We also need, perhaps to a lesser degree, MCSO deputies who may be present at various polling places and voting centers.

In addition, MCSO deputies escort the vehicles with ballots from various voting centers throughout the County back to the MCTEC. They will watch to ensure that no one tampers with the secure boxes, and oversee the secure removal of the boxes of ballots from each location, the safe transport across the cities, and the safe deposit inside the tabulation center.

As we will learn, with the increasing number of individuals who harass or threaten election workers, the MCSO may have to assign deputies to specific individuals to protect them from threatened harm.

It's actually a lot to do.

PART FOUR

THE 2020 ELECTIONS

"[T]his is a complicated country; there are more than
330 million people. And my mother used to say,
'It's every race. It's every religion'…
People have come to accept this Constitution and
they've come to accept the importance of the rule of law…"

—Supreme Court Justice Stephen Breyer, January 27, 2022,
announcing his retirement from the Supreme Court
from *The Big Truth: Upholding Democracy
in the Age of THE BIG LIE*
by Major Garrett and David Becker

CHAPTER 16

THE LEAD UP TO 2020

Our 21st century has seen more than its share of problems with, and threats to, our elections. From the time of our Revolution until the 2020 elections—over two hundred years—all election disputes have been resolved peacefully.

National Elections

In the 2000 Presidential election, Florida faced an unusual situation with computer voting, which led to the issue of "dangling chads." Did the computers count a clean vote on the ballot? The result was unclear, but if the plurality of votes in Florida went for George W. Bush, then the Electoral College count could give Bush the election. The U.S. Supreme Court settled the election in favor of George W. Bush. Apparently, Florida had followed its existing election laws. Contender Al Gore ceded to President-elect Bush, and we had a peaceful transition of power.

In reaction to the 2000 elections, Congress passed the Help America Vote Act (HAVA). Signed into law by President George W. Bush to make improvements to the nation's voting systems and voter access, HAVA created mandatory minimum standards for all states. It also established the Election Assistance Commission (EAC) to assist the states by creating voting system guidelines and operating the first voting system certification program.[25]

This program would involve trained experts in voting machines and systems examining the results of state and county elections to certify if they met national standards.

In 2008, when Barack Obama won the presidential election over candidate John McCain, McCain began his concession speech battling the rowdy booing of his anti-Obama supporters. In a show of great dignity and Constitutional acknowledgement, McCain raised his hand against the noise. He said that Obama had won, that he respected Obama, and that he would work with him for the good of the American People. Obama had clearly won, and McCain let his followers know that he accepted the vote of the American people. Again, there was a peaceful transition of the Presidency.

In 2016—during his presidential race against Secretary of State Hillary Clinton—candidate Trump started and repeated unfounded (actually false) rumors that the elections were "rigged" (his word) and the results would probably be fraudulent. He insulted his opponent by calling her "crooked Hillary." Despite the popular vote going for Clinton, when the Electoral College count went for Trump, he no longer called the election "rigged." It appears that to him, if he won, he would say it was fair, but if he lost, he would call it "corrupt."

That is not how our United States Constitution and laws operate, nor is it what they intend.

Although many people questioned the results in 2016, the evidence showed that Trump won the Electoral College vote count, as mandated by federal laws governing the process. (I don't quite understand them, but the people running the elections do.) Thus, similar to every candidate in United States history for over two hundred years, Clinton ceded to Trump and allowed the peaceful transfer of power.

Arizona Elections

Let's focus on Maricopa County, Arizona.

Helen Purcell became County Recorder in 1989. At that time, Maricopa County used punch card ballots. Purcell recognized that there was—and could be—a problem with punch-card ballots: witness the "dangling chads" fiasco in Florida in 2000.

In 1996, Purcell ordered a new scan-vote system. The machines were the early version of today's machines that scan the ballot, counting the voter's choices. Originally, voters signed into a physical Poll Book, which would record the voter's receipt of a ballot at that specific location.

Subsequently, new electronic Poll Book equipment allowed the signature to be scanned and sent to other e-Poll Book machines at other voting locations, preventing a voter from moving from one polling place to another to vote more than once. (This scanning and tracking system was not available in 1996.)

Meanwhile, the population in Maricopa County (and Arizona) was increasing rapidly, and Purcell recognized the need for new, better machinery. Unfortunately, the Arizona Legislature controlled the funding of the County elections budget, and it was underfunded for several years.

In 2016, Purcell faced several problems. The Recorder's Office reduced the number of voting centers due to limited funds. Further, the machinery for handling the elections needed updating.

There were two main kinds of machines: 1) the e-Poll Book, which recorded the voter's check-in and sent it to all other scanning machines at all other polling places; and 2) the tabulation machines, which had no electronic connection outside the voting center. Both needed to be replaced with newer, better, more expensive equipment.

Meanwhile, an elected state official allegedly announced on national news that "everyone in Arizona could vote" in the Presidential Preference election.

That was not true. Only individuals registered in one of the two major political parties (Republican or Democrat) could vote, and only for candidates within their own party.

But on election day, an extra 25,000 people showed up at polling places to vote. They had to be allowed to vote a provisional ballot, but they were also informed that their vote would not count. Each person had to be documented in the Poll Book. Long wait lines characterized that election day.

Finally, in violation of Arizona statutes, the Maricopa County Board of Supervisors had, for decades, given over its statutory responsibilities for elections. The BOS had let the County Recorder handle it all.

After the 2016 election, when Adrian Fontes became County Recorder, he worked to make the office more efficient and better serve all Arizonans who wanted—and were eligible—to vote.

Upon winning the election as County Recorder, Fontes set out to improve voting conditions. Meanwhile, the population of Maricopa County was growing fast, as was the number of registered voters. Fontes made some mistakes in how he planned and oversaw the 2018 mid-term elections.

Recognizing these challenges, the Board of Supervisors came to realize the seriousness of the problems and the implications of abdicating its own responsibilities.

While Fontes initially did not want to relinquish any authority, Supervisor Chairman Bill Gates negotiated a revised Elections Operating Agreement. They reorganized the Maricopa County Elections Department.

The County Recorder handled registered voter files, early ballots, mail-in ballots, drop-off sites, and early voting centers.

The Board of Supervisors and the Election Department, directly under their supervision, would manage in-person voting, Election Day voting, and the tabulation of ballots.[26]

By 2018, most of the county's voting machinery and equipment were obsolete, with numerous malfunctions.

In 2019, the Maricopa County Board of Supervisors invested in new Voting Tabulation equipment. They leased the equipment because they knew it might improve in the near future.

The new equipment was the Dominion Democracy Suite 5.5B, which Maricopa County officials first tested in November 2019 by conducting a mail-in-only election in the Madison School District.[27]

Leaders of the political parties learned of the November 2019 election through the local newspaper. Staff and members of both political parties conducted a Hand Count of one hundred percent of the ballots. Additionally, the county used the Dominion equipment to tabulate the vote. Both the machines and the Hand Count were a hundred percent match—they totally agreed with each other. The machines (and humans) made zero errors.

In late 2019, we were approaching a significant national election with a highly contested presidential race between then-Republican President Donald Trump and his Democratic challenger, Joe Biden, who had served as Vice President under Democratic President Barack Obama from 2008 to 2016.

Three separate elections were to be held during the 2020 election season in Maricopa County, beginning in March.

First, on March 17, 2020, was the Presidential Preference Election (PPE), an election in which voters could choose their preferred presidential candidate for the upcoming General Election. Official determination of Party winners of the Arizona PPE occurs at the party's national convention. Only voters registered within participating parties can vote in the PPE.

Second, in August, the State Primary Election was held. Only persons registered within the party affiliation could vote. Independents could vote if they registered with a specific party. They could vote on that party's ballot.

Third, on November 3, 2020, was the General Election.

On December 12, 2019, in preparation for the March 17, 2020, Presidential Preference Election, the Supervisors approved their original Election Day and Emergency plan. It included staffing forty "Vote anywhere" locations, where voters could cast their ballots early; hiring and training 1,500 poll workers; and increasing the number of check-in locations for Election Day from 120 to 240.

Maricopa County Recorder Adrian Fontes approved the Early Voting Plan. It included communication about the Voter Registration Deadline on February 18 (2020), making forty early voting locations available between February 19 and March 13, hiring new Voter Registration Clerks for all voting locations, and holding community outreach events to educate voters about key election information.[28]

At this point, in December 2019, no one knew that the COVID-19 pandemic would arrive in the United States in January 2020.

Most Americans were also unaware of the extensive planning efforts by then-President Trump to stay in power and sabotage the 2020 election if the win went to Joe Biden.

CHAPTER 17

EVERYTHING HAPPENING EVERYWHERE ALL AT ONCE

The content covered in the following six chapters was happening all at the same time.

While each event deserves a separate chapter, they are all related. Meanwhile, other things may be happening, such as our daily lives or world events.

As a brief preview, here are the six:

Ch. 18. Donald Trump was President, and he planned to stay in office regardless of the election outcome from the popular vote or the electoral college vote. He had won in 2016 only through our Electoral College system, because he had lost the full popular vote to Hilary Clinton by about three million votes. Trump wanted and planned to remain President of the United States.

Ch. 19. COVID-19, a new version of the Coronavirus—for which at first there was no vaccine for prevention or protection—landed on America's shores in January 2020. It was a huge and completely unexpected public health crisis.

Ch. 20. The election on November 3, 2020, in Maricopa County, Arizona, took place with people voting in person, many mail-in ballots, early ballots, ballots from overseas, and even a few Braille and "X" ballots.

Ch. 21. Public officials received threats during and after the election season.

Ch 22. Six individuals, all holding public offices and acting in their capacities as officials who had sworn to uphold the U.S. and Arizona constitutions and laws, maintained their integrity as human beings throughout. Regardless of whom they voted for in the election, they all fulfilled their responsibilities as elected officials. Four of them upheld the valid results of the popular vote. The fifth and sixth prevented a vengeful miscarriage of justice. They acted from 2019 through February 2021.

Ch. 23. Others, wanting Mr. Trump to win, created or believed alternate falsehoods and conspiracy theories.

CHAPTER 18

THE PRESIDENT'S PLAN
TO STEAL THE ELECTION

During the 2016 campaign of Clinton vs. Trump, evidence surfaced that Russia had attempted to interfere with the Presidential elections. That was true. There was evidence that Russian "troll farms" supported efforts to encourage angry, divisive protests in the U.S., both for and against racial justice efforts, such as Black Lives Matter.[29]

More importantly, cyberattacks originating from Russia gained access to some U.S. election infrastructure, notably the voter registration database run by the Illinois State Board of Elections.[30]

More troubling was abundant evidence that Donald Trump and several of his allies and members of his election team had close and positive relations with Vladimir Putin and others in positions of power in Russia. For example, throughout the 2016 campaign, Trump referred to Putin as "highly respected," and, when questioned by Bill O'Reilly about Putin being a "killer," Trump put the U.S. on the same moral level by saying, "We've got a lot of killers, you think our country's so innocent?"[31]

Why is this information so unsettling? With the brief exception of a partnership during World War II to fight Nazi Germany, the U.S. has been at serious odds with Russia, known for decades as the USSR. With the Russian revolution in 1917 and the emergence of the Soviet Union—Russia taking over neighboring countries by force— its brutality toward other countries and its own citizen dissidents is thoroughly documented. Vladimir Putin's actions are horrific and in total opposition to our principles of democracy, free enterprise, and equal justice for all people.

When a presidential candidate, who then went on to win the election in 2016, lavished praise upon a long-time enemy of our democracy, his behavior threw enormous doubt and uncertainty into our national psyche. It became clear that Mr. Trump was willing to support a ruthless tyrant, possibly at the sacrifice of democratic principles in the United States.

The 2016 election between Mr. Trump and Hillary Clinton exposed a further willingness to disrespect our Constitution and laws. For over two hundred years, all presidential candidates have ultimately agreed to the election results and the peaceful transfer of power.

While there have probably always been errors in the voting process, rarely has any proof of fraud, much less any error, changed an electoral outcome.

Americans do not like fraud. We have State and Federal agencies set up to protect against consumer fraud, including the prevention of selling contaminated food, recalls of potentially dangerous automobiles, and prosecution of phone call fraud and internet fraud. We do not like fraud.

Voting fraud has been almost—and increasingly—non-existent. Why? Because across the United States, election officials have tried to prevent and root out fraud, primarily through the effort to have both a Republican and a Democratic representative be present at virtually every stage of the game. This effort to prevent fraud has improved over the decades.

I've witnessed attempted fraud more than once.

Decades ago, in New York City, we discovered that the Italian-American Democrats were hiding the Chinese (Mandarin) language ballots and instructions to make it more difficult for Chinese-Americans to vote. This action was an attempt at fraud.

In 2020, I witnessed the then-President Trump's daughter giving a pro-Republican speech in the parking lot of a Democrat-predominant voting center. Because of the protection provided for the family of the President, a van from the Secret Service blocked the main entrance of the polling place's parking lot—in violation of Arizona law. This action, too, was an attempt at fraud.

In 2020, Mr. Trump repeatedly suggested that the election was "rigged" against him. When asked if he would accept the results of the election should he lose, he always refused to say he would. Instead, he said, "I'll keep you in suspense."[32]

He went on to say, "I would accept a clear election result, but I would also reserve my right to contest or file a legal challenge in the case of a questionable result." He said he would "totally accept the election results if I win."[33]

In making these comments, Mr. Trump, who had a loyal following, set in motion the idea of it being acceptable for the proven loser to challenge the winner.

However, our national Constitution, laws, and state Constitution and laws do not allow that. Our tradition of the peaceful transfer of power to the winner does not allow such a challenge. Even the peculiar custom of allowing a winner of the votes in the Electoral College to win while losing the popular vote does not allow that. Yet Mr. Trump planted the seed that he could do the unallowable—the un-Constitutional and the illegal. Many people seemed to come to believe it would be allowable to reject the legal election results!

At other levels, politicians and candidates alleged issues of fraud and conspiracies. In 2018, the Arizona GOP commissioned attorney Stephen Richer to conduct an "independent audit" of the 2018 election results. For example, their report included baseless insinuations about Adrian Fontes and George Soros, a Democratic fundraiser. Richer ran for County Recorder in 2020 against Adrian Fontes on the issue of potential voter fraud, "questions," and unsubstantiated election conspiracies.[34]

Nevertheless, the 2018 Maricopa County elections resulted in no fraud and no substantial questions.

In 2020, all during the year, Mr. Trump—who was still President while facing a tough battle against challenger Joe Biden—continued to indicate on Twitter posts that he might refuse to recognize the outcome of the election if he were defeated. In July, he declined to state whether he would accept the results and even suggested postponing the election due to the COVID-19 pandemic. He repeatedly claimed that if he lost, it was because the election would have been "rigged" against him and he would not agree to a peaceful transition of power. At one point, he said, "Get rid of the ballots and you'll have a very peaceful … there won't be a transfer, frankly. There will be a continuation."[35]

It turns out that a significant number of people worked outside the legal framework of our country—along with Mr. Trump—to prevent the peaceful transfer of power if Joe Biden won the election.

Trump and his allies repeatedly suggested the likelihood of fraud—the election might be "rigged."

Meanwhile, FBI Director Christopher Wray, a Trump appointee, testified under oath that the FBI had "not seen, historically, any kind of coordinated national voter fraud effort in a major election, whether it's by mail or otherwise."[36]

Even on the day after the election, Mr. Trump threw false claims out to the public. On Wednesday, November 4, at 2 am, with inconclusive election results trending in favor of Biden, Donald Trump held a press conference at the White House, stating, "This is a fraud on the American public. This is an embarrassment to our country… Frankly, we did win this election." On November 5, he tweeted, "STOP THE COUNT," even though the count had already given Biden a victory. On November 7, even after all major news organizations, including the pro-Trump FOX News, declared Biden the President-elect, Trump, who had lost the election, stated, "This election is far from over… I'm just not going to leave. We're never leaving. How can you leave when you just won an election?"[37]

When all the evidence was in, with clear results for Biden, Trump repeatedly refused to abide by the Constitution and laws of this country. He appeared to be living in an alternate reality. He was deliberately trying to steal the election.

Meanwhile, during the entire election season, Mr. Trump and the country were accompanied by the specter of death and disease with the spread of COVID-19.

CHAPTER 19

THE COVID-19 EFFECT

In January 2020, COVID-19 was virtually unknown in the U.S.

By March 3, the Centers for Disease Control and Prevention (CDC) reported 60 cases across Arizona and other states. By June, roughly 125,000 deaths had been reported in the U.S.[38]

In 2017, the Trump Administration had disbanded the White House pandemic response team. In January 2020, COVID-19 arrived in the U.S. On January 22, President Trump said, "We have it totally under control." However, on January 28, Trump's National Security Advisor told him, "This will be the biggest national security threat you face in your presidency." Despite the advice, on March 6, President Trump said, "It'll go away." On March 26, the U.S. became the country with the most confirmed coronavirus cases, and it remains the country with the most confirmed cases through Trump's time in office through January 2021.[39]

In Maricopa County, the Board of Supervisors received reports from the Director of the County Health Department. The threat of contagion was real, and people with underlying conditions were most susceptible. Public health professionals recommended the use of masks, frequent hand washing, and social distancing. Masks were already widely used in China, where the pandemic had taken a significant toll on the citizens, as well as in other countries.

On March 11, 2020, Arizona Governor Doug Ducey issued a Declaration of Emergency and Executive Order to Combat the Continued Spread of COVID-19 (on the following page, in part).

"The Coronavirus/COVID-19 situation is rapidly changing. Below are resources and links to help you navigate this time.

- We know that COVID-19 tends to affect older adults (over age 60) and those with underlying health conditions who are more vulnerable than other individuals.
- Staying home when you are sick helps individuals at greater risk reduce their exposure and their chances of becoming severely ill.
- Individuals who are at higher risk of illness due to age or underlying health conditions should make sure they have enough food, medications, and supplies in case they become ill and have to stay home.
- COVID-19 spreads through respiratory droplets when a person coughs or sneezes, spread through close contact, and within 6 feet for greater than 10 minutes.
- There is now community spread in Arizona, which means we have positive cases of COVID-19 [for which] we have not been able to identify the source of exposure, and there was no travel.
- There is currently no treatment or vaccine for COVID-19. Asymptomatic people do not require testing for COVID-19 because even if a test come[s] back positive, there is no change to the treatment protocol.
- To minimize spread, people should cover their coughs and sneezes and stay home if they are sick. People should also wash their hands frequently and not touch their face, where germs enter the body."[40]

There was more information, with links to the Arizona Department of Health Services, the U.S. Centers for Disease Control and Prevention, and the Maricopa County Department of Public Health.

Meanwhile, the Presidential Preference Election was scheduled for March 17. The Board of Supervisors met and discussed the risk of infectious disease to voters and all County personnel.

On March 13, Supervisor Bill Gates sent the following message:

Dear Friends,

In light of the rapidly evolving Coronavirus/ COVID-19, all District 3 Community Events are **CANCELLED through the end of March...**
And regarding the Elections:
Due to the COVID-19 pandemic, at the direction of the Board of Supervisors, the Election Department will be reducing the number of in-person voting locations from 229 individual polling locations to 151 'vote anywhere' locations due to poll worker attrition, facility closures, and a lack of cleaning supplies.
Please check the website,
Locations.Maricopa.Vote
[elections.maricopa.gov/voting/where-to-vote. html], for all open locations and your voting location, as it may have changed.
The Board of Supervisors held an emergency meeting last night [March 12] to discuss election options.

Our County Elections Department is preparing for the Democratic Presidential Preference Election next Tuesday and instituting procedures to keep polling locations sanitized. If you have received but not mailed your ballot, you must drop it off at a drop box, early vote location, or on Election Day, at a polling location or vote center.

Our Maricopa County Public Health Department is monitoring the COVID-19 situation closely and is sharing information as it becomes available on our website at Maricopa.gov/Coronavirus. I have included additional links and information below as well to help you prepare during this time. As a member of the Maricopa County Board of Health, know that I am monitoring the situation closely and will be sharing information as it is available.

All my best and stay safe, Bill.[41]

That was March 13. The election went forward on March 17. On March 20, Director of Election Day and Emergency Voting Scott Jarrett gave a verbal report to the Board of the required changes made to the election system for the completed Presidential Preference Election. The Board had given Jarrett five days to make changes in the number of polling places and vote centers, staffing changes, and sanitation efforts.[42]

The stress was enormous. In a matter of days, the number of available voting centers went from about 240 to about 40 to about 151.

Despite all the stress and chaos of COVID-19, the Presidential Preference Election went off without noteworthy problems.

The pandemic continued to get worse throughout the U.S., including in Maricopa County. On March 20, the AZ Department of Health Services reported the first COVID-19 death in Arizona. By June 8, 2020, there were 27,678 cases of COVID-19 in Arizona and 1,047 reported deaths.[43]

Hospitalizations and deaths due to COVID-19 were escalating. It was obviously a pandemic.

On June 18, Governor Doug Ducey issued Executive Order 2020-40 authorizing [but not mandating] cities, towns, and counties to adopt policies about wearing face coverings in public to slow the spread of COVID-19.

On June 19, the Maricopa County Board of Supervisors sent a mandate to every resident in the county. "Wear a mask no matter what city, town, or area you live in."[44]

The Board of Supervisors said it acted because the number of reported COVID-19 cases continued to climb. The Supervisors and the leaders across Arizona debated the practical issues of enforcement, the philosophical issues of public health and individual liberty, personal responsibility, and the reality that more people were going to die.[45]

Let's think about this situation.

The County Board of Supervisors heard from numerous city Mayors within the county that something drastic, such as mandatory masking, needed to be done. But they didn't want to do it because of too much opposition from people voicing concerns about their individual liberty, and politicians turning a public health issue into a political issue.

With a public health issue, in general, the concern for the good of the entire public may override an individual's right of personal choice. An example of governmental concern for everyone's health is the requirement of multiple vaccinations for children entering public school, despite some individuals' desire not to comply.

While many mayors thanked the Board, they would not publicly support the mask mandate. The BOS did what they believed was right, yet faced threats and criticism for doing so.

With this political and public health climate during the entire 2020 election year, you can see how it could be one of our "monsters"—too much horrible, serious information for us to cope with. But ultimately, with millions of people sick, hospitalized, put on ventilators, and dying, COVID-19 was real.

The COVID-19 crisis was only matched in intensity by the lies and misinformation put out by then-President Trump and his allies to cast significant doubt on the integrity of the election process in the United States and Maricopa County.

It's time, then, to look at what actually happened on Election Day, November 3, 2020, in Maricopa County.

CHAPTER 20

THE REAL 2020 ELECTION

As dawn was breaking on Election Day, November 3, 2020, hundreds of paid poll workers and volunteer observers got in their cars and fanned out across Maricopa County to cover every single polling place.

The work preparing for a successful Election Day began much earlier. County officials evaluated mistakes and miscalculations from 2016 and 2018. The Supervisors set the stage for Election Day when they selected the Dominion Democracy Suite 5.5B voting equipment in 2019. Why? Because Dominion machines were state- and federally-certified as high quality and capable of handling voter numbers of over one million voters.

Additionally, Maricopa County had used the Dominion machines for the 2019 Madison School District election. County officials completed a one-hundred percent hand count after using the equipment. Both the hand count and the tabulated results were a match—that is, zero errors.[46]

In 2020, before the Presidential Preference election in March, the August Primary, and the November 3 General Election, the County Election Department and the Secretary of State performed Logic and Accuracy (L&A) tests, as required by Arizona law. The purpose of the test is to confirm the correct attribution of votes to the candidates and ballot measures in the "election management system" (tabulation machines), and that each candidate and ballot measure receives the accurate number of votes.

Any chance of a one-party boondoggle?

The 2020 Secretary of State, Katie Hobbs, made sure that at least two election staff members of different political parties oversaw the L&A test. Furthermore, her office issued a public notice via a county-wide newspaper, the County website, and a media advisory invitation to the press, as well as to the three chairs of the county's political parties and the general public. All persons interested in the election knew about and were invited to witness the test, held on October 6, before the November 3 election.

Again, the election details are over my head. I don't know. It could be a giant conspiracy of the bipartisan election nerds, or (which I prefer to believe) it could be dozens of professionals who know what they were doing. Even though I don't know what they were doing, I trust them. Mainly because: 1) they're tech nerds; 2) the voting equipment was nationally certified by specialized certifying companies as accurate and up to the task of handling over one million voters; and 3) Republicans and Democrats watched the process—and each other—at every crucial step of the way.

Pretty serious testing rigor.

So, Election Day finally arrived. Keep in mind the many early ballots—both mail-in and hand-in at vote centers—and the ballots cast on Election Day. There were two sets of tabulators—the central count tabulators located at the Maricopa County Elections Department, for the early votes, and the Election Day tabulators in all the voting locations for in-person voting on Election Day. Between Recorder Fontes and his staff and the County Supervisors and their staff, including experts Scott Jarrett (Director of Election Day and Emergency Voting, who reported directly to the BOS) and Rey Valenzuela (Director of Election Services and Early Voting, who reported directly to the County Recorder), all machines had been checked (L&A) and placed where they needed to be to get the job done.

At least one Republican and Democrat were always present to make sure the other one doesn't cheat. I've been a polling place worker, and I've observed the scrupulous attention to the details we learned in our training.

I recall a specific day when I became acquainted with my coworker. Across the room, a paid poll worker started a loud rant about how the illegal Mexicans were coming over and illegally voting.

Never mind that there wasn't a "Mexican"-looking person in our polling place. Never mind that people who actually look for dirt on illegals voting have—repeatedly—not found it.

What mattered then, to us, was that the poll worker was violating the rules against any campaigning within 75 feet. We locked bipartisan arms and marched across the floor. "No sloganeering, or we call the boss and get you kicked out." Our bipartisan effort stopped the illegal behavior. That's a lot of how things operate inside the polling place. The predominance of multi-party workers ensures a safe and neutral voting environment for everyone.

One of the past voting problems had been "overvoting," when a person mistakenly votes for more candidates than allowed.

Largely because of the better equipment, fewer than 200 ballots had an over-vote in the presidential race on November 3. (There had been over 10,000 in 2016.) The new equipment made it easier for bipartisan-teamed poll workers to contact voters and/or hand-read ballots to clarify the intended vote.

Arizona law requires a hand count (an audit) of two percent of the Election Day ballots and one percent of the early votes. The Maricopa County Elections Department (Scott Jarrett, Rey Valenzuela, and their staff) conducted a hand count as required by law. Democratic and Republican party observers selected the early ballots included in the hand count on November 3.

That hand count qualified as an audit.

On November 4, the political parties conducted a second audit. The three political party chairs (or their appointed designees) did a random draw of the early ballot batches in voting locations included in their separate hand count audit, which did not include the staff of the Election Department. The result of this second, separate audit was a hundred-percent match of the hand count results and those produced by the tabulation equipment.[47]

Meanwhile, a Vote Count Verification Committee of statisticians and elections officials set the margins for a manual hand count. The trigger in Arizona law for the Presidential Election[48] as of 2014 and still in effect in the 2020 elections, was that an automatic recount would occur if there were a difference in the statewide vote count between the candidates of less than 0.1%. After the 2020 elections, the revised statute required a hand count or a recount when the margin is less than 0.5%.[49]

None of the counts met these thresholds (percentage of closeness in the vote count) on November 3 or 4, and so no extra hand counts or recounts were needed. The elections were accurate and fair.

On Election Day, Maricopa County used the Dominion Tabulation Equipment, similar ballot styles, and Sharpie pens with the quickest dry-time compared to other pens, so they would not bleed or mess up the ballot.

The political party appointees found zero variances between hand count results and the Dominion tabulation equipment.

After the equipment counted all the ballots, the County Elections Department completed a post-election L&A test on its equipment. That test found no changes made to any software throughout the election. It was the final step to verify election results.[50]

So that's pretty much it. Maricopa County officials conducted an extensive search and found excellent equipment—the Dominion Democracy 5.5B Suite—that kept testing at zero errors. Then they hired and trained staff. Poll workers showed up and did their jobs. Both major political parties, and sometimes all three (the Libertarians), were invited, present, and participated in selection of samples for the hand count, which they conducted themselves. Ultimately, it was a fair and accurate election.

CHAPTER 21

REAL THREATS AND DANGER IN 2020

We are not sure of the specific cause. Was it lies and disinformation about elections and candidates, primarily from Donald Trump and those supporting him? Or was it the COVID-19 pandemic that hit this country so rapidly? Was it general unease exacerbated by several factors? A general presence of mean-spiritedness?

Could it be that the President aimed to ridicule the elections? Did he know many average followers were ignorant of the complex election process, who, listening to the leader, would be willing to cast the first stone?

Trump's outcry against early voting led to almost 300,000 ballots in Arizona being dropped off on Election Day rather than being mailed in earlier or dropped off at Drop-Off Locations. Therefore, it resulted in a delay in the final count due to the time required to process these votes.[51]

It was clear that Donald Trump purposely sowed doubt about our institutions. During the entire 2020 election year, when he was still President and challenged by Joe Biden, he falsely claimed that mail-in voting caused fraud. Also, for the first time in U.S. history, he refused to commit to a peaceful transfer of power should he not win the presidential election.

"The simple fact is this election is far from over," said Mr. Trump on November 7, when the election results demonstrated clearly that Biden had won. He vowed to prosecute his case "in court to ensure election laws are fully upheld."[52]

While Mr. Trump did not say out loud, "Go out there and threaten people," his insults toward other individuals, claims of a "rigged election," and other false accusations about the election process encouraged a volume of threats from his allies and followers against election workers and their families.

From 2016 forward, threats against Maricopa County elections officials and staff steadily increased. In 2018, Recorder Adrian Fontes' daughter picked up an anonymous package left on the porch and brought it into the Fontes home. Fontes contacted law enforcement, and a bomb squad evacuated the Fontes family from their home. In the neighborhood, police ordered the evacuation of several adjacent homes before the bomb squad disposed of the object.[53]

In addition, during the November 2020 election, armed protesters marched in the streets. They stopped at the Recorder's office in an apparent attempt to disrupt and interfere with the Recorder's responsibility to count and process absentee ballots.[54]

With no proof of any wrongdoing by either the County Recorder or the members of the Board of Supervisors, in early 2020, threats, doxing (publishing private information of public figures), and online harassment began in earnest. The threats intensified and continued in toxicity through 2023. Mainly due to the strain of hatefulness, Bill Gates decided not to renew his term as supervisor.[55]

Meanwhile, in the spring of 2020, due to the severity of the COVID-19 pandemic threat, the Board of Supervisors, responsible for managing public health emergencies, had enacted a mask mandate. Far-right activists and average citizens, ignorant of the community-wide public health issues, apparently not concerned with our historic Constitutional tradition of balancing individual rights against public safety, called it a violation of their personal liberties.

One afternoon, Gates pulled into his driveway and checked his mailbox. There, he found a flyer with his face superimposed on a body holding a whip.

"This is your neighbor Republican Bill Gates, the District 3 Maricopa County Supervisor. He thinks he's your master…He wants you MUZZLED." His neighbors had also received the flyers.

One of Bill's daughters asked how people with such vicious tactics knew where they lived. Another was devastated that the flyer equated her father's support of the mask mandate to slavery. His third daughter couldn't sleep for several nights.

Gates told the kids not to open the front door and to keep a close eye on their surroundings. He began fielding phone calls and texts from neighbors about suspicious cars and strangers outside their home, including one who took photos. That summer, and several more times over the next two years, when far-right activists posted his personal information online, he or his wife would often rush home from their jobs to ensure that the girls were not alone.

The attacks worsened during the 2020 Presidential campaign. In the days before the General Election, Gates kept track of Trump's false attacks on mail-in voting, the charge that dead voters had cast a large number of the ballots, and that equipment used to count ballots was compromised. Republicans had initially favored mail-in voting, expanding its use in some states, such as Arizona, for decades, along with many other states, during the COVID-19 pandemic. None of Mr. Trump's claims had any evidence and were, in fact, untrue.[56]

Even with numerous and specific threats of danger, officials planned no extra security or protection for this election, as no one had required it in previous elections.

Recorder Adrian Fontes oversaw the counting of ballots in the MCTEC center on November 3 and several days following. Protesters gathered outside the building over the course of several days. Among them was conspiracy theorist Alex Jones. Fontes was worried that the protesters would storm the building and invade the ballot-counting area, potentially disrupting or preventing an accurate count of the votes. He met with the sheriff's department and other law enforcement agencies about establishing a secure perimeter around the property. They ultimately determined that there was no real threat to the staff or the building. However, due to threats against Fontes and his family, he secured a separate safe house, and they packed "to-go" bags; on one occasion, they even removed themselves to an undisclosed location.[57]

Indeed, from the onset of early voting for the 2020 Presidential Election, the level of threats of violence against staff and civil servants who administer elections in Maricopa County increased. Out of hundreds, the Arizona State Joint Terrorism Task Force considered thirty-five severe enough to investigate.

Scott Hadley, the deputy County Recorder for Operations during the 2020 Election, as well as being a career military officer and lifelong Republican, said,

> The potential was there for anything to go wrong…
> My biggest regret was that we had to do this at all, just
> to get through the election, to let civil servants do their
> job and run an honest, fair, and transparent election.[58]

The fuller picture included more threats, which continued after Election Day and persist to the present day.

First, let's learn how the actions of six men stopped the steal.

CHAPTER 22

HOW THE SIX STOPPED THE STEAL

It was as simple as each one of these six showing up to do the job that they had sworn they would do. As Bill Gates later said, "It was really a no-brainer." However, in 2020, many steps and decisions culminated in the Supervisors certifying the vote count; the Speaker of the House, Rusty Bowers, refusing to call a special session to change the vote; and Arizona Senator Paul Boyer casting the final vote against a motion for contempt that would have jailed all five Supervisors.

Before November 3

In practical terms, the fact that Democratic County Recorder Adrian Fontes and the Supervisors (four of whom were Republican) agreed to work together to make Maricopa County's voting system the best it could be at every turn set the groundwork for an extremely well-run set of three elections in 2020.

First, in 2019, Fontes and the Board haggled over and ultimately agreed on their Elections Operating Agreement, which later became known as the Shared Services Agreement. Fontes relinquished some of the responsibilities that a previous Board had surrendered to the County Recorder's office, thereby ignoring Arizona law. In 2019, Fontes and the BOS all agreed to restore those duties to the proper authority—the Board of Supervisors.

Second, the Board agreed to try Fontes' suggestion of voting centers where anyone could vote once and have their vote recorded by computers that could also verify the voter information. This agreement allowed people to vote whenever and wherever they had time. Many people voted early, either by mail or at open voting centers. The presence of centers being open for weeks ahead of Election Day resulted in reduced lines at polling places, almost eliminated provisional votes—all of which have to be hand counted—and streamlined the voting process.

In 2020, the Board of Supervisors and the County Recorder were ready to do their jobs.

In March, under enormous pressure from the COVID-19 outbreak, the Presidential Preference election was successfully conducted, despite the strain of last-minute cancellations and the challenge of finding new voting center locations.

The fact that COVID-19 necessitated social distancing and sanitation made the voting center system even more valuable. With virtually no lines in the many days in which people could vote, voters could distance themselves, wear a mask, and remain almost completely risk-free of the disease.

That election went off well.

The August Primaries, likewise, went off well.

On October 6, 2020, the Maricopa County Logic and Accuracy test was completed with a notice published. As in 2019, the political parties had been notified and invited in September to observe the L&A test. The BOS and County Recorder supported and oversaw the carrying out of these responsibilities.

Then came the General Election—the election in which President Trump was being challenged for the next term.

Maricopa County voters had access to vote at home, as well as in-person voting, beginning 27 days before November 3 (Election Day), and included special election boards for individuals with various special needs and for emergency voting.

The robust mail-in-ballot system, which had been in place in Maricopa County for several decades, resulted in higher Democratic turnout in the PPE in 2020 than in 2016. Nearly ninety percent of Democratic voters voted early, either by mail-in ballots or through dropped-off ballots.[59]

November 3 and 4—Election Day, Night, and the Morning After

All of these election actions were dress rehearsals for November 3—General Election Day. Supervisors doing their job ensured that everything up to the General Election worked properly. They needed to know that at every step of the way, the election process was free, fair, confidential, secure, and transparent. They would all need to know with great certainty that the elections were done without any fraud and with virtually no errors.

The Supervisors spent their time during the General Election in various ways. While Recorder Fontes was at the MCTEC Center, overseeing the ballot counting, protesters surrounded the building, and he consulted with the MCSO on what to do.

Supervisor Jack Sellers spent the night at home. Because he was on the ballot, MCTEC was off limits. His Chief of Staff instructed him to stay somewhere completely safe while he monitored everything and would inform Sellers if he needed to address any problems.

"It was a frustrating time, during a pandemic, to be so focused on ensuring that the election was done right and having people in my own party questioning what we were doing."

Supervisor Clint Hickman was home the night of November 3, fatigued from running three elections during COVID-19, yet also happy to hear of only a few operational difficulties.

Bill Gates watched the results at home on TV. "It was surreal, because when I went to sleep, I was trailing my opponent by 19,000 votes. I eventually caught up to her and was re-elected."

By November 4, when major media called the election for Joe Biden and the results from the Maricopa County tabulations gave the majority of votes to Biden, Trump's allies almost immediately began trying to convince Gates, Sellers, and Hickman to stop counting votes and delay certification of the results.

Bill said, "One of the first calls was from AZ Republican Party Chair Kelli Ward, who texted me and asked me to call Sydney Powell. I never called Sydney…"

Jack commented, "I don't remember how soon after Election Day I started getting calls from party leadership. Early on, most were from Kelli Ward, who had names of people she wanted me to call. I stopped answering calls from her."

Reply from Clint: "My phone started ringing with gusto the next morning [November 4], led by Kelli Ward and other 'champions' of Trump."[60]

After The Election—The Actions That Stopped the Steal

The Board of Supervisors, determined to ensure that the votes were tabulated correctly, held a special hearing on November 20, within the statutorily mandated time frame, to canvass and certify the General Election results.

Clint Hickman had taken over the position of Chairman of the BOS from Bill Gates in January of 2020. On November 20, it was Clint's job to take a position of leadership on the matter of the Canvass and Certification of the election results. With enormous pressure coming from calls from Trump supporters—fellow Republicans who must have known they were asking the BOS to violate their oath and break the law—Hickman and all the other Supervisors asked numerous questions of Election Directors Scott Jarrett and Rey Valenzuela at the November 20 Certification hearing.

The meeting took over two hours and 45 minutes. Chairman Hickman and the supervisors listened to the extensively detailed report by Jarrett and Valenzuela. They asked every possible reasonable question that had come before them. Jarrett and Valenzuela provided evidence and gave answers to every question, supporting the accuracy of the election results. By November 4, it had become clear that the elections were not going the way Mr. Trump wanted. Questions and accusations from pro-Trump followers bombarded the BOS.

In an attempt to bring some reason to the voting public, especially within his own (Republican) party, Hickman wrote his first letter to the voters on November 4. Both he and Democratic Supervisor Steve Gallardo signed the letter in an effort to show clear bipartisan support for the bipartisan work of the BOS, the County Recorder's Office, and the Elections Department.

Unfortunately, the false accusations continued.

Hickman knew the results of the election before November 20. On November 17, he again wrote to the voters of Maricopa County.

> Dear Maricopa County voters,
>
> Members of the Board of Supervisors continue to hear from government leaders and the public about the integrity of Maricopa County elections. We want to assure you that proper steps have been taken to ensure a full and accurate count of all votes.
>
> Here are the facts:
> The evidence overwhelmingly shows the system used in Maricopa County is accurate and provided voters with a reliable election. On Election Day, fewer than 200 ballots had an overvote on the presidential race out of more than 167,000 ballots cast on Election Day.
>
> The Dominion tabulation equipment was vetted by a bipartisan 'Equipment Certification Advisory Committee' before the contract was finalized. As required by law (A.R.S. § 16-442), the committee

tested the functionality and accuracy of tabulation equipment before it was used in any Arizona elections.

The Dominion tabulation equipment met mandatory requirements during Logic and Accuracy testing before the Presidential Preference Election, the Primary Election, and the General Election. And after each of these 2020 elections, the hand count audit showed the machines generated an accurate count.

Last week, the Elections Department conducted the mandatory hand count of Election Day ballots from two percent of vote centers and one percent of Early Ballots as required by Arizona law and it yielded a hundred percent match to the results produced by the tabulation equipment. All three political parties participated in the hand count audit. This is a statistically significant sample of thousands of votes, which would have caught irregularities.

There are triggers in Arizona law to require another hand count or even a recount in the case of a close contest. None of those thresholds have been met during the 2020 General Election.

More than two million ballots were cast in Maricopa County [in early voting] and there is no evidence of fraud or misconduct or malfunction. Board members listened to and considered many theories about the election results. We asked, and continue to ask critical questions of County staff and none of these theories have proven true or raised the possibility the outcome of the election would be different.

The Board is required to canvass the election by November 23, 2020 (A.R.S. § 16-642). It is time to dial back the rhetoric, rumors, and false claims. I appreciate the efforts of our elections staff who worked tirelessly to run this election during a pandemic. No matter how you voted, this election was administered with integrity, transparency, and in accordance with state laws.

Thank you,
Clint Hickman, Chairman,
Maricopa County Board of Supervisors[61]

The Supervisors Vote

Four of the five supervisors were Republican, and most of them acknowledged that they had voted for Trump and were personally disappointed in the Presidential election results.

But their legal responsibility as Supervisors was to oversee the election and canvass (scrutinize) the results. If they believed the election results were fair, secure, and accurate, their job was to certify the results.

Finally, satisfied on November 20 by the Report from the Elections Department that all his questions had been resolved—with clear evidence that Joe Biden had won the Presidential election—BOS Chairman Clint Hickman made a statement to the rest of the Board that he was satisfied with the results of the post-election audits. He would be voting to certify the election. Each of the five supervisors made a statement about the election and praised the work of election staff, poll workers, and volunteers.

Supervisor Jack Sellers made a statement about the election being one of the best-run ever and made a motion to certify the results. Bill Gates seconded the motion. On a request for all in favor, the five Supervisors unanimously voted "Aye."

Five votes stopped the steal.

Keep in mind that the sitting United States President insisted that the election was "rigged" and that he was the real winner. Keep in mind that many of his supporters, sincere or otherwise, had begun to harass and threaten the County Recorder, each of the Supervisors, and many election staff. Numerous phone calls and emails threatened bodily harm to them and their families. Keep in mind that four of the five Supervisors were Republican, had been friends with or befriended by the sitting President, and probably voted for the man who—they realized—lost.

On that very day, November 20, Kelli Ward, who was then Chairman of the Arizona Republican Party, called Bill Gates to implore him to delay certification.[62]

Was the vote of the five Supervisors to stop the steal of the 2020 Presidential Election—by then President Trump and his supporters—a holy moment? Were the later actions by Rusty Bowers and the "no" vote by Paul Boyer also holy moments?

Indeed, it was a moment when each of these men aligned their lives and their integrity in how they handled the 2020 election. Bill Gates compared their Constitutional duty to uphold the election results to the experience of his grandfather, who "went to Europe to fight for democracy" during World War II.

To me, it appeared to be fierce courage. Each one did what they knew to be the right thing in the face of enormous and hostile opposition from their own Republican Party members (for most), and even threats to their lives and the lives of their families.

Yet to several of them, it was a "Duh." Gates said, "Of course, we would do what was right, both personally and because it was our oath to uphold the law." At the same time, he said, "Clint's leadership by writing a letter outlining the clear reasons for certifying the election results provided the guidance that made it easier for all of us to also do the right thing."[63]

County Recorder Fontes never voted, but he did his job, and he improved the handling of the elections dramatically from blunders in 2018 to an excellent performance in 2020. The Republican supervisors, who would have certainly held him to account had there been any problems, said that he had run an excellent election. He and the Supervisors had all upheld their oath of office and done their job.

Even then, the BOS ordered an independent audit so that an outside, unaffiliated set of inspectors would confirm or deny the results. The Supervisors were determined to expose their own work to outside auditors to ensure the validity of the results they fully believed were accurate and fair.

Pressure From Arizona Republicans

Once the election results were clear and the national results announced, the pro-Trump forces launched an intense effort to get the Arizona Legislature to reverse the vote, or to decertify the appointment of Biden-bound electors and replace them with self-appointed pro-Trump electors.

Rusty Bowers was Speaker of the Arizona House of Representatives. Several Arizona Legislators wanted Bowers to join them in suing MCTEC. He said no. He had been at the MCTEC for three to four hours (on Christmas Eve, no less). They had videotaped the voting. Bowers knew the procedure certified by the BOS was accurate and complete. The Legislators did not sue MCTEC.

Arizona Congressmen Andy Biggs and Paul Gosar told Bowers, "We have proof, there were 280,000 votes missing, there were irregularities from voting by mail."[64] They showed Bowers an Excel spreadsheet.

But Bowers saw that the spreadsheet was not from the County elections. He knew that an MCSO deputy sheriff had been in each truck that transported ballots to the tabulation center and had signed off on the proper delivery of all the ballots. The County had gone through all the steps. The Biggs video of a spreadsheet was one of seven or eight random documents from a company in New York City whose business received data from around the world and then filled orders to receive and send documents.

It was not a certified election document. It was a random paper with columns A & B. It was not from Maricopa County. Bowers also knew that Biggs' and Gosar's claim that the Sharpies had bled through ballots was untrue. What Biggs and Gosar said about stolen votes was a lie. Bowers would not participate in suing the County.

Meanwhile, a group of Arizona Republicans, including Arizona GOP Chairwoman Kelli Ward, signed a false document that sent a slate of fake electors for Trump to Congress. That violated Arizona law and the Constitution.

Pressure from Trump and Giuliani

Pressure came from the top as well. On November 22, 2020, two days after certification, Bowers received a phone call while driving. The message said, "White House." President Trump came on the phone, and they exchanged pleasantries. Then Giuliani got on the phone to tell Bowers of alleged evidence of fraud.

Bowers said he needed to see the evidence on his desk before acting. Trump told Giuliani to "give the man what he wants." Bowers never saw any proof. "Not then and not a week later, not two weeks later, not now. Never," said Bowers when asked if he had ever received any proof.

But Giuliani also asked Bowers if he would present this "evidence of fraud" in a formal hearing at the Arizona House of Representatives and then use it as justification to call the legislature into special session and decertify the election results. Bowers responded, "I am not going to have a circus."

Bowers told Giuliani that the Arizona Legislature would need votes from Democrats in order to go into special session. Lawmakers can convene a special session if there is a two-thirds majority of both the House and the Senate. That was not going to happen.

Instead of ever bringing evidence, Giuliani kept up the pressure. After an informal hearing at a Phoenix hotel, Giuliani brought five Arizona Republican Senators to the Senate caucus chamber on December 1. At that meeting, Giuliani asked Bowers and those present to call a special session to decertify the results of the election. Bowers did not let it happen.

But the pressure continued. Trump called Bowers shortly before Christmas. It seemed "surreal," because Trump just said, "I want you to know that I appreciate your support and the work you did for the campaign, and I just want you to know I'm grateful and wanted to thank you personally."

Bowers said to Trump, "I cannot and will not entertain a suggestion that we violate current law to change the outcome of a certified election."[65]

Right up to January 6, 2021, Republicans pressured Mr. Bowers. On the morning of January 6, U.S. Representative Andy Biggs called Bowers to ask him to consider decertifying the electors. Again, Bowers refused to break his oath to the Constitution and do something against the law.

Rusty Bowers was the only Republican in the Arizona House who refused to cooperate with what he saw as illegal conduct. Bowers had voted for Trump, and yet he knew that the results for a Biden victory were accurate, true, and fair. He would not violate his oath to God and the Constitution for politics.

Pressure from the Senate

The Senate Republicans were not finished with the BOS.

They seemed to be on a steamroller course to deny the truthful results of the election to keep Mr. Trump in power and—for the first time in American history—prevent the peaceful transfer of power to the actual winner of the election.

In one last effort to challenge the Supervisors, the Senate subpoenaed all the ballots and equipment from the General Election. In early February, the BOS had asked the Superior Court for clarification on the validity of the Senate's subpoena. On Wednesday, February 3, before the scheduled full Senate meeting the following Monday, the Republican Caucus met in private. They discussed a Resolution to hold the Supervisors in contempt for their refusal to deliver all ballots and equipment from the General Election. The contempt resolution could land all five Supervisors in jail for as long as the rest of the legislative session—up to six months.

Paul Boyer, a seasoned member of the Arizona House, had been recently elected to the Senate on November 3. As Boyer saw it, the situation was both tense and hectic. About 1,500 bills are introduced into the legislature each year. Some move on, others do not. Boyer could not afford to support his family on only the $24,000 legislator's salary, so he was also a school teacher. That meant he taught school every morning, then rushed over to the legislature to attend meetings, read up on bills, and go to the Floor for debates on bills and "3rd Read" votes. As such, he did not have time to read up on every bill thoroughly, knowing that only one in five of the bills introduced would ever make it to the Governor's desk.

Boyer expressed reservations. The Chief of Staff to the Senate President advised him to go along with the majority of his party and to consider his relationships with his colleagues.

There was also the issue of the House Rules Committee Chairman being able to hold up—and not move forward—any bill that Senator Boyer introduced during that legislative session. Boyer knew that this one "no" vote could hold up all of his bills—all of the other good work he was doing for his constituents and his district.

Boyer wanted to work well with his fellow Senators. And yet, he kept one Bible verse on his desk that continually spoke to him: "For am I now seeking the favor of men, or of God? Or am I striving to please men? If I were still trying to please men, I would not be a bond-servant of Christ." [Galatians 1:10, in the New American Standard Bible (1995).]

On Wednesday, Boyer signed on to the Resolution S.R. 1005 to hold the BOS in contempt.

Signing on to a bill or resolution does not mean voting for or against it. It indicates support for the bill proceeding to a vote. Boyer signed to move it forward.

However, this Resolution did not sit right with Paul Boyer. That weekend, the weekend of the Super Bowl, he was on a retreat with his church group. Although the Resolution was not a topic of conversation at all, his mind kept turning S.R. 1005 over and over. It did not feel right to him.

The Senate Republicans seemed determined to jail six elected officials for refusal to turn over all ballots and machines—even though the Senate admitted that they had no space available to receive the materials they had subpoenaed.

One thing kept resurfacing. Boyer had run across a piece by a columnist for whom he had great respect—*Arizona Republic* columnist Robert Robb. Robb wrote the following about the Senate's contempt proposal: "Senator Republicans only have a one-vote margin. If there is any Republican in the caucus with a shred of judgment and conscience left, now is the time to stand up and put an end to this travesty." Robb had gone on to say, "It is a travesty what the Senate is doing. Is there one Senator who will speak the truth?" [66]

Robb did not mention him by name. However, Paul thought that Robb was speaking directly to him.

Super Bowl Sunday arrived. Boyer called Senate President Karen Fann and BOS Supervisor Bill Gates, asking them to meet as elected officials only, with no staff, on Monday morning to work it out together, just the three of them.

Boyer had read A.R.S. § 41-1153 and A.R.S. § 41-1155, regarding disobedience of a legislative subpoena and the potential amount of jail time.

In good conscience, Boyer believed that the Supervisors deserved time to resolve the matter in court, that the accusation against them was improper, as well as unprecedented.

They met in Fann's office on Monday at 8:00 am. Fann urged Boyer to go along with the majority of his party. Bill Gates said, "My daughter asked, 'Dad, when are you going to jail?'"

Said Boyer, "That's when it hit me. It's nuts to jail someone, elected or not, for following the law." When the Senate met for the vote at 1:30, Boyer was the only Republican to vote "no."

That one Republican vote saved five men from six months of jail time—men who had upheld Arizona law and adhered to their conscience and oath of office.

The Six

If you count all the votes, the total is seven. But one supervisor's vote is not being counted here because of his later conduct. A few months later, Steve Chucri betrayed his colleagues by saying untrue and insulting things about them—to some staunch Republican pals.

Someone in that private group publicized the tape of that conversation. Once outed, Chucri did acknowledge his lapse of integrity, apologized, said that they were "good men," and resigned from his elected position on the Board. For that, he deserves credit.

If Steve Chucri had shown genuine resolve to adhere to principles of integrity, we might have counted his vote. But when they knew the candidates for the newly vacant BOS seat, he chose to endorse an irresponsible party-pal instead of a man of experience and integrity.

There is no mistake. The vote was fair, secure, and accurate. The votes in Maricopa County went—by a legally solid margin— for Joe Biden. Trump and his supporters were willing to violate the Constitution and break the law to obstruct the peaceful transfer of power. No matter what they said, they were trying to steal the election from the duly elected candidate, Joe Biden.

So, by February 2021, six elected officials were left standing—five of them Republican—who could be counted as persons of integrity. These six men stopped the steal.

CHAPTER 23

ALTERNATE REALITIES, CONSPIRACIES, AND BULLYING

After Donald Trump's allegations in 2016 that the election might be rigged if he did not win, he made the same false claims during 2020.

Even with widespread allegations of fraud, Trump and his allies provided no evidence.

Before the November 2020 election, key Trump supporters organized efforts in several competitive states for an alternate set of electors who could vote for Trump even if Biden won.

The night of the election and within hours of the polls closing on November 3, Trump allies promoted false information about "Sharpie Gate," a conspiracy that claimed the use of Sharpies by voters at polling places would cause a miscount of the ballots due to ink bleeding through paper on a two-sided ballot. QAnon followers, who falsely claimed that Mr. Trump "is battling a cabal of satanic pedophiles," rallied in the County MCTEC parking lot and demanded entry into the building where authorized staff worked inside to count and process ballots. The protestors chanted, "Let me in!" and demanded that Recorder Fontes come outside.[67] According to Fontes, a former U.S. Marine with marksmanship teaching experience, many appeared armed with AR-15 assault rifles. The following night, conspiracy theorist Alex Jones made a "surprise appearance," and, using a megaphone, urged all protesters to "surround the White House and support the President."[68]

According to Hickman, "I was on my couch when Fox called the AZ race for Biden, shocked because I knew that the lead was going to shrink. My phone started ringing with gusto the next morning, led by Kelli Ward and other 'champions' of Trump that wanted to be visible as they started their stabbing the backs of Republicans that had anything to do with supporting our election staff."[69]

Immediately after the election, Trump's allies tried to convince the Supervisors to stop counting votes and delay certification results. The President's supporters sent an avalanche of emails and phone calls to probe false claims, including the claim that large numbers of ballots had been cast on behalf of dead voters (there were none) and that the equipment used to count ballots was compromised.[70] Several tests proved that the equipment was not.

On November 20, the same day that the BOS met in a special hearing to receive the full report from Scott Jarrett and Rey Valenzuela of the Elections Department (under the BOS and County Recorder), Kelli Ward—Chairman of the Arizona Republican Party at the time— called to implore Bill Gates to delay certification. As a high-powered member of Bill's own political party, she should never have made that call. It was bullying and inappropriate—and very probably illegal— conduct. She knew—or certainly should have known—that it was his Constitutional duty to certify the results if he saw them to be accurate.

Gates held to his integrity. He knew his oath of office; he knew the law. As an attorney, he provided some legal leadership to the other BOS members. Despite the pressure, the BOS certified the results.

Threats to all Supervisors, the Recorder, and other election personnel mushroomed.

On December 2, 2020, Sidney Powell (a Trump attorney) filed the lawsuit *Bowyer v. Ducey* on behalf of 14 people, 11 of whom went on to become fake electors. The suit sought to decertify the election of Biden or to certify Trump's electors. The suit and its appeals were dismissed or rejected all the way up to and including the United States Supreme Court.

On December 14, 2020, Arizona's legitimate electors (based on Biden's victory) met to formally cast their ballots for Biden, which is typically a procedural formality. Eleven Arizona fake electors, designated by the Republican Party as the slate for Trump, gathered at the Arizona Republican Party headquarters in Phoenix and signed a certificate falsely asserting that they were the "duly elected and qualified" electors. They purported to cast the state's electoral ballots for Trump.

Also in December, twenty Arizona legislators "signed a resolution attempting to get Congress to accept eleven alternate electoral votes for Donald J. Trump—a staggering act of defiance of the people's will."[71]

The Arizona Republican Party promptly posted a video of the signing on social media, including Twitter. They sent the fake electors' certificates to Congress and the National Archives, which did not accept them because they were not valid.

On Christmas Eve 2020, then-President Donald Trump's attorney, Rudy Giuliani, called Bill Gates to try to change the election results in Arizona. The voice mail from Giuliani said, "Hey, Bill, I have an idea how to fix this. Call me anytime…" Gates did not pick up, and he did not call back. Giuliani made the same call to Vice-Chairman of the BOS Jack Sellers and left the same voice mail. The President of the United States' attorney was using the full power of the Presidency to bully the Board of Supervisors to somehow stop the legal process.

In an effort to ensure election integrity—also on Christmas Eve—Bill asked House Republican Rusty Bowers to please come to the MCTEC Center and review the voting process. They spent four hours examining and clarifying the election process. They knew the results were accurate.

Thus ended 2020.

PART FIVE

THE AFTERMATH

"You know who will see whether that experiment works?
It's you, my friend…
It's that next generation and the one after that—
my grandchildren and their children.
They'll determine whether the experiment still works."

—Supreme Court Justice Stephen Breyer, January 27, 2022,
announcing his retirement from the Supreme Court,
from *The Big Truth: Upholding Democracy
in the Age of THE BIG LIE*
by Major Garrett and David Becker

"Believe in truth.
To abandon facts is to abandon freedom.
You submit to tyranny when you renounce the difference
between what you want to hear and what is actually the case."

—Timothy Snyder
On Tyranny: Twenty Lessons from the Twentieth Century

CHAPTER 24

THE SUPERVISORS CONTINUE THEIR AUDITS

A. November 2020

On November 20, 2020, the Elections Department officials provided a thorough, two-and-a-half-hour report to the Maricopa County Board of Supervisors. The Board members asked every question they could think of, including many from constituents. Scott Jarrett and Rey Venezuela answered all their questions thoroughly. The BOS unanimously certified the November 3 election results.

In December, at the request of a Republican and in cooperation with a court order, the BOS initiated another vote count. The results showed no fraud or change of election results.[72]

But the matter did not end there.

B. The Maricopa County BOS Commissions a 3-Part Audit by Independent Auditing Companies

On January 27, 2021, the BOS voted unanimously to authorize an independent forensic audit of the ballot tabulation equipment used in the 2020 elections. This audit was the culmination of a year-long effort by the County to ensure the accuracy of the federal- and state-certified hardware and software used to count votes.

This audit basically validated the accuracy of the equipment and processes used during the 2020 Election Year. This multi-layered forensic audit, comprised of three separate audits performed by two different laboratories, was certified by United States Election Assistance Commission, plus a similarly certified and experienced public accounting firm.

Two independent Voting System Testing Laboratories—unrelated to the County, a political party, or any candidate—performed the equipment audit: Pro V&V and SLI Compliance. They completed their report on February 23, 2021.

The third, separate audit, was undertaken by the certified public accounting firm, Berry Dunn. It reviewed the County contracts with Dominion Voting Service to verify that the BOS leased the tabulation equipment according to state and county procurement regulations. They completed this audit at the end of July 2021.

The auditors—Pro V&V and SLI Compliance—were certified Voting System Test Laboratories and, at the time, their certification was in good standing with the U.S. Elections Assistance Commission.

The Supervisors asked the auditors to review and analyze the tabulation source code and perform the assessment necessary to identify vulnerabilities. Using a certified Voting System Test Laboratory is essential, as it is the only firm with the combined skills and knowledge to verify that the configuration of the systems meets federal certification standards.

The Department of Homeland Security-designated tabulation equipment is critical to election infrastructure. If the source code is exposed and posted online, it could compromise the integrity of voting systems across the entire nation.

Voting machinery and related computer programming are, for me, a "monster." The complexity and skill boggle my mind. But because they have worked so hard, and because all the firms involved were certified through a process at the state and federal levels, I consider it a safe space in which to think that the information they offer is accurate and way above the ability of either me or the folks who take pot-shots to undermine their credibility. If you haven't walked in the footsteps of Pro V&V, SLI Compliance, or Berry Dunn, you don't have the right to make false allegations.

Since Maricopa County faced more scheduled elections in 2022, it had to ensure that the tabulation equipment would remain certified as accurate and properly functioning.

The results of these audits included:

1. Pro V&V and SLI Compliance found that all software and equipment they inspected were using certified software and were not modified.
2. Pro V&V and SLI Compliance found no instances of malicious software or hardware installed on the tabulators or system.
3. Pro V&V and SLI Compliance found no evidence of Internet connectivity.
4. Pro V&V (only within Pro V&V's scope of work) found no evidence of vote switching. The equipment had tabulated and adjudicated ballots accurately.

Some questions—malicious or sincere—arose that the BOS knew they had to answer. Here is how the audit results answered these questions.

1. Were the Auditors certified?

Yes. Certification is a specific process conducted by experts to ensure that the auditors have the necessary skills, knowledge, and ethics to perform audits properly.

2. Was the audit superficial, at the surface level?

No. They were thorough. The auditors took apart the tabulation equipment piece by piece to the core components. They traced the core components back to the certified design-build, ensuring that no one had installed foreign hardware.

In the software tests, auditors took a bit-by-bit clone of the devices, as well as every event log and audit log of the system.

They used five different antivirus and malware forensic examining tools to scan the bit-by-bit clone and search for any malicious software or viruses.

These scans would have detected whether any device was connected to the Internet or an external USB drive was plugged into the election equipment.

The testing was so thorough that when the Elections Department compiled the data and logs for the Arizona Senate's subpoena, the Senate-contracted auditors (Cyber Ninjas) were able to see exactly the steps taken.

3. Did the auditors hire some Dominion Employees?

No. They attested that they did not hire any current or former employees of Dominion voting systems.

The U.S. Elections Assistance Commission provides hiring restrictions for certified Voting System Test Laboratories. They would bar an employee hired from a former voting system from the development and testing of the equipment of their former employer for at least three years.

4. Did any current or former Dominion employees work at the audit firms hired by Maricopa County?

No.

5. Why is it essential for the software and hardware to match federal certification standards? What security tests were performed when the equipment was certified initially?

Maricopa County wanted to ensure that the equipment did not allow for vote manipulation, external or backdoor access, or any other hackable workaround.

Federal security standards include:

1. Protect critical elements of the voting system;
2. Establish and maintain controls to minimize errors;

3. Protect the secrecy of the voting process; and
4. Protect from fraud, intentional manipulation, malicious mischief, fraudulent or erroneous voting system changes.

6. Why did Maricopa County not audit the ballots?

The Board of Supervisors had conducted two audits in November and December 2020. As of January 2021, all of the ballots were sealed.

No provision under Arizona law allowed the County to "recount" or "audit" the election results after they were certified, which the BOS did on November 20, 2020. The County could not access the ballots—including digital codes—without a court order.[73]

7. Why did Maricopa County provide a public wireless network?

So that customers, including candidates and voters, can access the Internet while doing County business.

The tabulation equipment was an air-gapped system, meaning it had no access to any wireless network, including public networks.

The two Voting System Test Laboratories confirmed that the tabulation systems were a secure, closed network.[74]

Despite this thorough independent audit, other Republicans in the Arizona Legislature continued with separate audits.

On February 23, 2021, Scott Jarrett, Maricopa County Director of Election Day and Emergency Voting, and Rey Valenzuela, Director of Election Services and Early Voting, provided their report to the Maricopa County Board of Supervisors. It was called the Update of the Forensic Audit.[75]

Jarrett's report summarized the results.

The first test objective was to determine if the installed software was certified by both the AZ Secretary of State and the U.S. Election Assistance Commission. The Pro V&V field audit found that all tested software and equipment were inspected and verified to be using certified software. The SLI Compliance Forensic Audit showed that all tested systems and equipment were using certified software.

The second objective was to determine if any malicious malware or hardware was installed on the system or equipment. Pro V&V's field audit found no malicious hardware or software discrepancies were identified. The SLI Compliance forensic audit found that no malicious malware or hardware was detected.

The third objective was to determine if tabulators were connected to the Internet. Pro V&V found that the system was a "closed network" and did not have Internet access. SLI found no evidence of an Internet connection.

The fourth objective was to perform a Logic and Accuracy test to determine if vote switching could occur. Pro V&V's field audit found that the L&A test resulted in accurate numbers. SLI's audit did not include this test within its scope of work.[76]

In July 2021, the Berry Dunn CPA reported to the BOS. Their question was: Did the Office of Procurement Services (OPS) of the County conduct the procurement and award the contract (to Dominion Voting System, Inc., in 2019) with integrity, honesty, and fairness, and in accordance with the Maricopa County Procurement Code and County Procurement Procedures? (My eyes glazed over while I was reading this question!)

Berry Dunn found that OPS did conduct the solicitation and award of the Elections Tabulation System in a fair and ethical manner that was transparent and in accordance with all the requirements of state statutes and the Maricopa County Procurement Code. Berry

Dunn found a few minor informalities that had no impact on the solicitation or reward.

In simpler language, the OPS solicited bids for the job more broadly. Three certified systems labs applied for the contract to do the work. Dominion was chosen from a fair, competitive bid process.[77]

C. Independent Investigation and Report on 2022 General Elections

In 2023, the BOS asked Former Arizona Supreme Court Chief Justice Ruth McGregor to do an independent investigation of the November 8, 2022, General Election. Some of the older printers (not the Dominion tabulators) could not maintain the required temperature to consistently print ballots dark enough to be read by the on-site tabulators.

Judge McGregor's investigation included extensive interviews with County staff and contractors, followed by the printing and tabulating of 9,100 ballots on randomly selected printers and tabulators.

The cause of the "equipment failure" was in some of the County's Oki B432 printers, which had more difficulty with longer ballots (20 inches vs. 19 inches) and were printed on heavier paper (100 lb. vs. 80 lb.) This problem occurred even though the same printers performed well in the August Primary Election and pre-November stress tests with 20-inch ballots on 100 lb. paper. At that time, tests resulted in no problems. In the end, despite some voter frustration, all voters were able to cast their ballots and all legal ballots were counted and included in the county's results.

On April 10, 2023, the Board of Supervisors reported that the investigation was complete. Chairman Clint Hickman said,

> "I pushed for an outside investigation as soon as this happened, and I appreciate Justice McGregor and her team's thorough, professional and independent review.

We don't grade our own homework and now that we have a better idea of the factors involved, we'll make changes to best serve voters, starting with replacing some equipment."[78]

<h1 style="text-align:center">CHAPTER 25</h1>

<h1 style="text-align:center">THE REPUBLICAN LEGISLATURE
CONTINUES ITS INVESTIGATIONS</h1>

A. Republican Re-Count, November 2020

On November 30, 2020, a Maricopa County Superior Court Judge had granted a request from the leader of the Arizona Republican Party to inspect a sampling of 100 Arizona ballots for irregularities. The Republican Party then returned to court and asked to review more ballots, and the County (at that time) said it would not object.

The two Republican reviews of more ballots did not find irregularities in vote counting significant enough to change the outcome of the November 2020 election.[79]

B. Arizona Senate Judiciary Hearing: December Subpoena and January Subpoena

On December 14, the Arizona Senate Judiciary Committee plus one held a hearing to require answers from BOS Chairman Clint Hickman and Elections Director Scott Jarrett. The hearing lasted nearly six hours.

Although Hickman and Jarrett answered all questions raised on December 14, former Senator Farnsworth sent a subpoena to Maricopa County (the "December Subpoena") requesting millions of documents from Maricopa County.

The subpoena demanded that the members of the BOS provide the people's ballots and federally-certified election equipment, as they said, "sufficiently in advance of the congressional review of the Electoral College returns on January 6, 2021,"[80] a move that some

Republicans thought would have allowed Congress to misrepresent the actual, accurate vote of the Arizona people.

The County sought guidance from the Superior Court, believing the subpoena was not properly issued and that the command to disclose certain materials violated state and federal law.

On January 12, 2021, at 4:00 p.m., the Arizona Senate Judiciary served the BOS with a second subpoena, commanding the appearance of the newly-elected BOS Chairman, Jack Sellers, the Maricopa County Treasurer John Allen, and the Maricopa County Recorder Stephen Richer, at 9:00 am on January 14. Upon their arrival there was no hearing, but a Senate staff person told them to leave the documents. They delivered many documents on January 15.

However, the BOS believed some requests were ambiguous and requested clarification from the Arizona Senate's lawyer and then sued in Superior Court to get a clear court ruling.

C. The Senate Contempt Resolution and Court Ruling

The January 2021 subpoena threatened to jail the Supervisors for contempt if they did not comply.

On Wednesday, February 3, the Senate Republican Caucus met to decide whether to hold the Supervisors in contempt. One Senator, Paul Boyer, was concerned. He said that he felt that the BOS was acting in good faith and the Senate should not act on the motion for contempt. It carried a possible jail sentence of six months, the length of the time the Senate might be in session. Upon advice, Boyer signed the Senate Resolution with all other Republicans. That would be enough—with all Democrats voting no, to carry the motion for contempt.

On the morning of February 8, the Arizona Senate was set to vote to hold the Supervisors in contempt if they did not comply with the Senate subpoena for a massive number of documents and machines from the General Election.[81] The Senate knew it had no space to receive the ballots and machines it demanded.

Supervisors Bill Gates and then Chairman Jack Sellers went to the Legislature on Monday to lobby against the Senate move. They believed that Arizona law prohibited them from providing the sealed ballots without a court order.[82] Gates and Sellers were fully prepared to be jailed for their conscience rather than break the law as they understood it. They were awaiting a decision from the Court.

Only the "no" vote of one Republican Senator—Paul Boyer—stopped the Senate from holding members of the BOS in contempt and sending them to jail. He had reconsidered his position and believed that to hold the BOS members in contempt was wrong. There was a majority of "no."

Gates sent a text to his family that he would not be going to jail after all.

Within a week, Boyer received over 20,000 hate-messages by phone or email condemning him for voting according to his conscience. This matter was finally resolved in Court, as such conflicts should be.

The County believed that the multiple audits already conducted by the County were sufficient, and the November 2020 ballots—audited twice—must remain sealed, according to state law. The Senate argued that they needed another audit and a thorough review of the already audited information.

On February 26, Maricopa County Superior Court Judge Timothy Thomason interpreted Arizona law. He ruled that the subpoenas issued by the Arizona Senate—challenged in court by the Maricopa County BOS—were valid. He ordered the BOS to hand over the ballots and equipment from the election, which it did.[83]

The judge stated that the ballots from the November 2020 General Election had to be turned over to the Arizona Senate, and the Senate had to be provided access to the County's voting machines, so it could conduct an audit. "The Senators, of course, are obligated to maintain confidentiality of the materials tried over to them. Confidentiality, however is not a basis for quashing the Subpoenas."[84]

BOS Chairman Jack Sellers responded the day of the Court decision—three days after the Report on completion of the separate BOS-contracted audits by Pro V & V and SLI Compliance. The County would immediately start working to provide the Senate with the required materials. Sellers said, "We hope Senators will show the same respect and care we have for the 2.1 million private ballots and use them in service of their legislative duties."

Senate President Fann also responded to the Court order on February 26 that "It was never about overturning the election. It was about the integrity of the Arizona election system. If people have questions, they deserve answers."[85]

D. Arizona Senate Hires Cyber Ninjas for Another Audit

Meanwhile, in January 2021, the Republicans in the Arizona Senate with Karen Fann, President of the senate, also voted to hire an outside firm to conduct an extra-legal re-count of the ballots in Maricopa County. That firm was Cyber Ninjas, a Florida-based firm that was publicly pro-Trump, with no experience in election auditing and was not federally certified as competent to do the job they were hired to do.

Between late February 2021—when Cyber Ninjas started working for the Senate—and September, top Trump boosters and conservative influencers traveled to Phoenix to watch the review, even though this "audit" would have no power to change the outcome of the elections.[86] All the ballots were delivered to a place finally secured in March by the Senate—the Veterans' Memorial Coliseum in Phoenix.

By subpoena, the Senate took possession of 2.1 million ballots and nearly 400 elections machines and turned them over to be Cyber Ninjas. Its CEO, Doug Logan, had touted theories of fraud in the Georgia and Pennsylvania elections and claimed that Dominion Voting Systems' core software originated from the intellectual property of Smartmatic, which was linked to the (long-dead) Venezuelan dictator

Hugo Chavez. Logan had tweeted, "I'm tired of having people say there was no fraud. It happened. Its real, and people getter get wise fast."[87]

Cyber Ninjas changed its policies and procedures, chased conspiracy theories, and spread false claims. They undertook a full hand-recount and review of the ballots and voting machines. At one point, they accused the BOS staff of deleting files that Cyber Ninjas simply could not find. It was one example of Cyber Ninjas' either knowingly lying, or exhibiting extreme incompetence.[88]

On May 12, in support of Cyber Ninja activities, Senate President Fann wrote a letter to the BOS and also tweeted several accusations. She included the allegation that Maricopa County deleted "a directory full of databases from the 2020 election cycle days before the election equipment was delivered to the audit," and she accused the County of "spoliation of the evidence." These accusations were false. See Ch. 27, May 17, 2021, letter to Fann.

In July 2021, Congressional House Oversight Committee leaders (Carolyn Maloney, D-NY and Jamie Raskin, D-MD), sent a list of concerns to Doug Logan of Cyber Ninjas—they sought records and called him to testify before the Committee.

On September 24, 2021, after much delay, Cyber Ninjas gave its report to Congress that Joe Biden had beaten Trump in the Presidential election by 360 more votes than had previously been reported. It upheld the validity of the general election results certified by the BOS, and affirmed that Joe Biden was (even to this pro-Trump firm) the winner of the election.

Meanwhile, detailed communications between Logan and national Republican figures and Trump allies, plus information about fundraising efforts for the review process, had been made public. The Arizona Senate sought to prevent either the Senate or Cyber Ninjas from having to release additional records.

But on September 14, 2021, Arizona Supreme Court Judge Maria Elena Cruz said that additional records about the review and its contractors should be released, because the records were subject to public records law since the contractors—Cyber Ninjas—were performing a government function.

"Allowing the legislature to disregard the clear mandate of the (public records law) would undermine the integrity of the legislative process and discourage transparency, which contradicts the purpose of both the immunity doctrine and the (public records law)."[89]

E. Attorney General Mark Brnovich Investigates the BOS Following the Cyber Ninja Report

Republican Attorney General Mark Brnovich did not investigate the illegality of the December, 2020, self-appointment of "fake" Republican electors from the 2020 election, which, as Attorney General, he could and should have done.

However, in October 2021, within days after the publication of the Cyber Ninja Report showing no evidence of fraud by the County in the 2020 elections, Brnovich launched an investigation into Maricopa County's administration of the election, including issues raised by the Senate's review. It appeared that these issues had been resolved by the Cyber Ninja Report, but a probe was begun nonetheless. The probe carried a new risk for all five of the Supervisors: an indictment for felony crimes.[90]

Such an extra investigation, from AZ Attorney General, Mark Brnovich, who took the same oath as an attorney and the same oath of office as Bill Gates—to uphold the Constitution and laws of Arizona, had every appearance of political-based, biased harassment and intimidation. For, as it turned out, that investigation soon resulted in findings that nearly all claims of malfeasance were unfounded, and the probe ended without any prosecutions in 2023.[91]

Nonetheless, in November 2022, Brnovich did bring an appropriate separate case indicting Peggy Judd and Tom Crosby, Republican County Supervisors in Cochise County, AZ, for conspiracy and interference with an election officer. They were obligated by law through the Arizona Constitution and their Oath of Office to canvass—scrutinize and certify—the votes from the Cochise County November 2022 election within the Arizona statutory deadline for doing so, and they had refused.[92]

F. The Kelly Townsend Subpoena

In March 2022, Arizona Senator Kelly Townsend sent yet another subpoena regarding the 2020 election. Her move was made after the County's own audits and reports—and after the report by the Republican Legislature-hired Cyber Ninjas in September, 2021—had all been made public and had shown virtually no error, no fraud, and only a few votes that would not change any election result.

Maricopa County Supervisor Bill Gates responded by saying that Maricopa County had already provided thousands of documents, data, and equipment to the Arizona Senate regarding the 2020 election. In February, the county produced over 4,400 documents to the Attorney General's office.

Gates pointed out that:

> Senator Townsend's subpoena [the Senate had discovered that it did have a powerful, Court-supported right to subpoena records] specifically references a "study" conducted by Shiva Ayyadurai that points to voter signatures and ballot envelopes which **are not public record.** [Emphasis NHM]. This is surprising because the County has not released this protected voter information to any organization other than the Arizona Senate following subpoenas in 2021 [which was admonished by the Court and by Supervisor Jack Sellers at the time to be respectful of private voter data], and the Senator is using the discredited work of Ayyadurai as a basis for this new subpoena. Perhaps Senator Townsend should suggest the Election

Integrity Unit (EIU) ask these questions of Arizona President Fann and "audit" subcontractors:

1. Why were voter signatures posted online, which is a possible violation of A.R.S. § 16-168.F?
2. Did the Senate's subcontractor notify the plaintiffs within 48 hours of the signature comparison as required by a settlement agreement in the Maricopa County Superior Court *(Arizona Democratic Party, et al. v. Fann)*?
3. How is comparing signatures from one unrelated public recorded document to an early ballot signature considered a viable way of proving identity for voting purposes?"

These questions don't even begin to address the faulty data extrapolation used in the [Ayyadurai] report. Given the number of false and misleading claims issues in EchoMail [Inc.]'s September 2021 reports to the Senate, it's not surprising this more recent report also uses faulty analysis to draw the conclusions desired by Mr. Ayyadurai.[93]

The Townsend subpoena was dropped.

G. The Committee on Oversight and Reform of U.S. House Of Representatives, and AZ Congressman Andy Biggs, Question BOS

After the October 7, 2021 hearing, at which Bill Gates and Jack Sellers gave testimony, the Committee and Biggs directed even more questions at the BOS.

On November 1, 2021, the County provided written responses via email messages.

1. "What were the results of the two independent audits of Maricopa County's selections that were conducted by firms certified by the United States Election Assistance Commission?"

   County: "There were three separate audits, Pro V&V and SLI Compliance; and Berry Dunn, an accounting firm. Pro V&V and SLI concluded that Maricopa County's election equipment and software passed all tests performed by these firms.

   "They confirmed that the equipment had not been connected to the Internet during the 2020 General Election, that no malicious software or hardware had been installed, that the tabulation equipment had not been hacked, and that the equipment was accurate and programmed so that a vote switching could not occur.

   "Berry Dunn CPAs conducted the procurement audit and found that the solicitation and award were fair and ethical and transparent, and they observed that it met all state requirements."

2. On July 15, 2021, Cyber Ninjas claimed, "We have 74,243 mail-in ballots, where there is no clear record of them being sent?"

   County: "This claim has been widely proven to be false, by the County, independent fact checkers, and the Cyber Ninjas themselves."

3. From Rep. Mike Quigley, keeping in mind the federal funds going to Arizona:
   a. "What are some shortcomings in the Arizona selection system that the funds could address?"

      County: "Have the federal funding go directly to Maricopa County rather than the Secretary of state—who must submit a spending proposal to an increasingly partisan legislature—so that the County can be sure to provide resources for hiring and compensating temporary workers, and for advertising to inform voters in every County."

b. "Did the Arizona Senate's audit meaningfully evaluate the shortcomings?"

County: "The Senate Audit by Cyber Ninjas was not meaningful at all."

c. "How did the audit itself risk or breach the security of Arizona's election system?"

County: "The chain of custody of the machines was broken when the senate subpoena mandated transfer of the equipment. The Cyber Ninja volunteers and other staff were not U.S, Arizona, nor County Election Officials. They potentially allowed inexperienced partisan actors to obtain proprietary information."

Questions from Republican (and election-denier) Andy Biggs:

1. "Is it standard practice to delete files off of a server after an election? Why was data still present from the prior elections?"

County: "Maricopa County did not delete the system or files. All the backup hard drives and associated data files have been maintained and safely secured." [The County report provided an even more detailed explanation.]

2. "How could the auditors validate the 2020 election results if the database was actually cleared before they got started?"

County: "The Senate's contractors had all the information they would need through a combination of the items they subpoenaed and received."

3. "Does the County change its election management system passwords?"

County: "Claims that Maricopa does not change passwords for election tabulation equipment are false. There are many other security measures in place as well." [Listed by the County.]

4. "Was only VoteSecur paper utilized in the 2020 general election?"

County: "VoteSecur paper was used for every ballot issued to voters during the November General Election, including overseas ballots. Other locations use other types of paper for non-ballot functions."

5. "What about County's slow response to Senate December 2020 subpoena and others?"

County: "Maricopa County began complying immediately, and wrote a letter to the Senate asking for clarification on some items. After no response, the County asked a court to rule. After the Court's ruling, the County turned over nearly 2.1 million General Election ballots, 385 Election Day tabulators, nine central count tabulators, and more than eight terabytes of election related data. The Arizona Senate acknowledged that the County has fully complied with the Senate subpoena."[94]

H. Another Senate-Generated Investigation of County Elections Equipment From 2020

In March 2023, despite the completion of the audit by of the Arizona Senate-selected "auditor"—inexperienced and publicly pro-Trump—the Arizona Senate decided it needed a new investigation of equipment. As per an agreement between the Arizona Senate and Maricopa County,[95] a Special Master—Former Republican Congressman John Shadegg—was designated by the parties to review and answer certain questions posed by the State Senate regarding conduct of the 2020 General Election.

Let's pause again. It would probably help if we understood computer systems—especially election systems—better. It would probably all be good if we personally knew the players involved. But we don't. We do know that Mr. Shadegg was acceptable as an independent investigating Special Master to both the BOS and the Senate, which was investigating the Supervisors for the third or fourth time after several pro-Republican and independent audits had been conducted. Realistically, all the relevant questions about the 2020 election questions had already been answered.

At issue were the routers and Splunk logs in the County's election network.

Maricopa County had taken this case to Court, believing it did not have the right or authority to hand over certain records or materials. Ultimately the parties agreed to limit the inquiry to "the County's routers and Splunk logs as they relate to the November 3 general election, specifically from October 7 through November 20, 2020."

The questions presented by the Senate were:

1. Were the routers or managed switches in the election network connected to the public Internet;
2. How were the routers and managed switches in the election network secured against unauthorized or third-party access; and
3. Whether routers or Splunk logs contained any evidence of data deletion, data purging, data overwriting or other destruction of evidence or obstruction of the audit; and further,

4. Whether any of a list of 57 separate "outputs" and specifically listed factors "supports or undermines" the answers to the Senate's three questions.

The Special Master's report provided these answers.

1. There is [and was] **no electronic connection between the BTC (Ballot Tabulation Center)—** the tabulator of election results only—**and the outside.** (This BTC was physically and electronically separated from the outside, monitored 24/7, and accessible only by authorized personnel with card key access.) There is [and was] no electronic connection between the BTC and the MCTEC [Maricopa County Technical and Election Center].

2. There are [and were] **no routers in the BTC.**

3. **No Splunk logs** were available for review of the BTC network within the MCTEC **because none were generated** as described above.

4. **The Voter Registration database** (from the OET—which exclusively stores and maintains registration records and information only—is **never transmitted to the BTC**, in accordance with the privacy provisions of the Arizona Constitution.

5. **Vote tallies,** as they are completed, **are loaded on a newly opened USB** (thumb drive), under the observation of politically appointed observers, **and then physically taken out of the Ballot Tabulation Center and loaded on a separate computer for distribution to the press and public.**

6. **The official canvass is also loaded on a (separate) newly opened USB and is hand-carried to the Secretary of State's office, along with chain of**

custody control documentation. The USBs taken out of the BTC are loaded on **separate computers, and the information is disseminated to the Secretary of State's office and to the Maricopa County website.** They are then returned to the BTC and saved for historical purposes.[96]

CHAPTER 26

THREATS, LIES, TRUTHS—2020 AND 2021

2021
Threats

On January 6, 2021, the speech by President Donald J. Trump shook this country to its core, as he urged his followers to march on the Capitol, followed by the violent break-in by rioters in an attempt to stop the election and the peaceful transfer of power. Never in over 200 years had a President refused to allow the peaceful transfer of power to his victorious successor. Never before had a President or candidate refused to accept the valid results, instead continuing to spread lies and false allegations.

And yet, some could not believe the facts and they called it "a peaceful day," the smashing of windows, the desecration of the building's interior, even the killing of some police and participants, and the call for "Hang Pence!" The dichotomy of announcements was startling and unbelievable.

In January of 2021, when Rusty Bowers refused to violate his oath and to unilaterally reconvene the Arizona Legislature in order to set up a vote to de-certify the bona fide Biden electors, pro-Trump protesters doxxed Bowers, sharing his private home address on social media. They called him a "traitor." Armed groups went to Bowers' home in Mesa. They set up video trucks and used blaring loudspeakers, falsely accusing him of being a corrupt politician and a pedophile.

Meanwhile, a fringe group, the Patriot Party Arizona—a failed political party—ran a recall campaign against Bowers. (It failed.) The group also protested numerous times outside the Bowers' home.

The protests began shortly after the election and continued into 2021. In one instance, an armed man sporting a "Three Percenter" logo stood on Bowers' property yelling at his neighbors. One of his neighbors was hit with such force by a protester's vehicle that it flipped the neighbor up onto the hood. The protester drove off.

"I never felt that I was in imminent danger, per se," said Bowers, "but in those situations all it takes is one of them to think, 'I'm going to prove that I'm a great patriot and so I'm going to pull out a gun and shoot this guy.'"

Bowers' home was the center of nine total protests, one of which occurred just before Christmas, when he was at his nearby church for a Nativity event. As the convoy with Trump flags headed toward his house, he called his wife at home and told her to contact the Maricopa County Sheriff's Office.

Bowers said, "It made me upset that they would harass my family. Who are these people that they would do this to America? Is this what civil discourse means nowadays? Have we gotten so bad that we have to act this way?"[97]

"I saw someone with a pistol, and my neighbor had gone outside to tell them to be quiet and stop disturbing the neighborhood. She didn't realize she was in danger. It isn't a good idea to be 20 feet away from a pistol. I went out and stood right near him, so I could grab the gun if I had to. The protestors and their trucks seemed to have lookouts posted, because when I called the sheriff, all of them left by the time deputies arrived."[98]

Meanwhile, threats against each Maricopa County supervisor have persisted. Like Bowers experienced, someone also doxxed Bill Gates. One emailer labeled him a traitor who should be shot or hanged. Another wrote on social media that someone should rape his daughters.[99] It was clear that some groups knew the private home address for Gates.

In November of 2020, shortly after the election results were certified, Trump-inspired loyalists showed up at Supervisor Clint Hickman's home while his wife and children were inside.[100]

Hickman told his teenage son he was going out to confront them and stand up for the fact that he had upheld the truth about the election. However, MCSO Sheriff's deputies persuaded Supervisor Hickman to stay inside with his family while they, law enforcement, dispersed the hostile crowd. He chose to respond to the hatred not with violence but with a quiet presence. "My son understood me," said Hickman.

2021
Lies and Threats

On July 22, 2021, then former President Trump issued a statement condemning AZ Senator Paul Boyer, "a RINO if ever there was one… doing everything in his power to hold up the damning Forensic Audit of Maricopa County…. He's being primaried…"[101]

In the fall of 2021, a few days after the release of the Cyber Ninja audit that confirmed Biden won the 2020 election, Mark Rissi of Cedar Rapids, Iowa—one of many Trump supporters—left Hickman a phone message: "I am glad that you are standing up for democracy and want to place your hand on the Bible and say that the election was honest and fair. I really appreciate that. When we come to lynch your stupid lying Commie ass, you'll remember that you lied on the f—king Bible, you piece of s—t. You're gonna die, you piece of s—t. We're going to hang you. We're going to hang you."[102]

Here is what one "monster" is for me. So many people were connected to Mr. Trump—co-planners or simply avid followers, both lying and conspiring to prevent, then overthrow, the results of the 2020 election—that I can't handle it. Having been educated in these United States to believe in the rule of law, I can't understand how many people were so fanatical about one man that they seemed determined to throw over 250 years of our history, Constitution, and democratic rule of law. But it's true.

Ongoing 2020 to Present Lies, Plans, and Truths

Here's a short list of several individuals who were intent on denying the U.S. Constitution and keeping Trump in power either by lies or by force. They are listed in order of appearance in *The Big Truth.*

1. Patrick Byrne alleged "industrial scale vote flipping," [untrue] and later wrote a book about his efforts to *overturn* the 2020 election results.

2. Peter Navarro, the White House trade advisor, claimed the election was lost due to "ballot box stuffing," which he knew was a lie. He wrote a book about *his* efforts to overturn the 2020 election.

3. Mollie Hemingway argued that the election was not stolen; instead, that it was "rigged" by hostile media coverage.

4. Ashli Babbitt was one of the vandals who charged the Capitol building, and the Capitol police shot her while defending members of Congress during the riot as she tried to enter the building illegally.

5. John Eastman, a Trump attorney, was a major planner of the overthrow of the election results, running a "coup in search of a legal theory." He claimed that Pence had the authority to ignore the Electoral College votes and deny Biden the presidency. In a memo, he stated that "Seven states transmitted dual slates of electors." He knew that was a lie.

6. Rick Perry, former Trump energy secretary, wrote, "Send our own electors."

7. Mark Meadows, White House Chief of Staff, in multiple texts and documents, *planned to prevent the lawful transfer of power.* He worked with Pete Navarro and Steve Bannon to enlist over one hundred House Republicans and eleven U.S. Senators to seek a delay in the January 6 certification of the votes by the presiding Vice President, Mike Pence.

8. Donald J. Trump, Jr. texted Meadows, "We have multiple paths. We control them all," and made the false statement on November 6, 2020, that we've "uncovered evidence of fraud."

9. Then-President, and then ex-President Donald J. Trump, himself, spread disinformation and doubt before the 2016 and 2020 elections. On November 3, 2020, he said, "They are trying to STEAL the election. We will never let them do it." After the election, he claimed they had stolen the election. He repeated this lie multiple times. Even in 2022, when visiting Arizona, he lied, "We had a tremendous victory in Arizona. It was taken away… the proof is all over the place." False, false, false. In early 2022, Trump considered using the military to seize ballots. As late as June 2025, he tweeted that the DOJ should appoint a special investigator into the 2020 elections.

10. Sidney Powell, Trump's attorney, lied about Dominion Voting Systems and was ultimately sued by Dominion. She and Mike Flinn told President Trump he "had power he was not using."

11. Senator Mike Lee, Republican from Utah, said at one point, "We have enough evidence to put everyone in prison for life, three-hundred-and-then-some million people." [Huh?]

12. Rudy Giuliani called and tried to influence Supervisor Gates, and knowingly submitted false allegations about Dominion Voting Systems.

13. Mike Lindell, the "My Pillow" guy, promised "proof of massive fraud," alleged that China had "switched votes," and also defamed Dominion Voting Systems.

14. Virginia Thomas, wife of Supreme Court Justice Thomas, attended the January 6 rally and sent Mark Meadows a text: "Biden crime family being arrested." It was completely false. She texted White House Chief of Staff Mark Meadows at least twenty-nine times, urging him to use all available While House resources to overturn Biden's election.

15. Former New York Police Commissioner Bernard Kerrick affirmed that part of the post-election-defeat strategy was to harass election officials—such harassment in Maricopa County during and ever since the 2020 elections is well documented.

16. Phil Waldon falsely claimed that China infiltrated the Dominion machines, hacked the election, and flipped votes.

17. Mike Flinn, along with Sidney Powell, told Trump he had power he was not using—encouraging him to go outside Constitutional guidelines.

18. Russell Ramsland, Jr., was hired by Patrick Byrne to "reverse engineer" and to "mislead people into believing the 2020 election was rigged."

19. Texas Republican representative Louie Gohmert voted against the certification of the votes from Arizona and Pennsylvania, and he sued Pence for not stopping the accreditation. The suit was dismissed.

20. Jeffrey Clark, the Assistant Attorney General for the Environment and Natural Resources Division in Trump's Justice Department, said he was eager to investigate, instigate, and invalidate, and knowingly wrote a false memo that the DOJ had "identified significant concerns," after the Attorney General, William Barr, had gone on record that the DOJ had found no fraud.

21. Elmer Steward Rhodes, founder and leader of the Oath Keepers, actively planned to stop the lawful transfer of power. He amassed almost $10,000 worth of firearms, including AR-platform rifles. On December 22, 2020, he said, "We will have to do a bloody, massively bloody revolution against them."

    On January 6, in response to a text that "antifa" had taken the Capitol, he responded, "I'm right here [at the Capitol building]. The patriots are taking it into their own hands."[103]

The Congressional investigations of the January 6 riots found original texts by some of these players that showed a coordinated plan to prevent the peaceful transfer of power on January 6, and, subsequently, to disrupt democracy by continued lies and harassment of election officials.

Here are some lies that Mr. Trump and his team have perpetuated in the last decade—and come of the truths countering them.

Lie

1. Trump alleged massive fraud through mail-in ballot voting. This allegation was false.

True

Trump only alleged fraud when the mail-in ballots seemed to weigh in favor of more Democratic votes. He did not complain in 2016 when Republicans used mail-in ballots and he went on to win the election.

The truth about mail-in ballot voting is that it has been used in the U.S. for many decades. Affluent Republicans initially favored it, and multiple safeguards are in place to prevent fraud.

Here are a few checks against fraud with mail-in ballots:

1. A voter must specifically request a mail-in ballot. That request is checked against the voter registration database to confirm the voter's eligibility and that the information on the ballot request matches the information on file.
2. Mail-in ballots are coded on the exterior mail-in envelope. Election officials use the code to verify that only official ballots are used, and they know exactly who has received a mail-in ballot. The voter's database is updated. If that person attempts to vote in person, they will either have to surrender their mail-in ballot or cast a provisional ballot, which will be counted only if the mail-in ballot is not received by the deadline.
3. Once received, the signature on the envelope is checked against the signature(s) on file. Only then will the mail-in ballot be processed for tabulation— that is, be counted.

Try defrauding your election system using a mail-in ballot and see how far you get.

Lie

2. Trump spread the lie about inexplicable "ballot dumps" early on the morning of November 4, 2020—specifically in Democratic areas, where the numbers against him did in fact rise. He falsely insinuated that the "dump" of ballots was somehow crooked, a plot to rig the election against him.

True

Fact: The large batches were, in fact, explicable.

There are large numbers of ballots often delivered and reported in batches. These batches come from larger voting centers, with several hundred ballots per batch. Election officials keep these batches together for more secure checking and double-checking.

Fact: In some states, election laws did not allow mail-in ballots to be counted until Election Day, resulting in batches being collected and held. In other states, election official counted early mail-in ballots as they arrived, and thus avoided the appearance of "ballot dumps.'"

More interesting facts: Election Day and other in-person ballots are usually the first reported, and they verify the voter at that time. Mail-in ballots are validated twice—once when the voter requests the ballot and then again when the ballot is returned—before tabulation.

In sum, while sometimes unavoidable "batches" of ballots arrive and are counted, they are not suspicious "dumps."

Lie

3. The Trump team falsely claimed that election officials excluded observers from their campaign were from watching the counting of ballots. They knew this was false.

True

Every state allows duly qualified observers from the campaigns and parties to observe the polling places and vote counting, as required by Arizona law and the *Election Procedures Manual.* There were verifiable Republican (and Democrat, and often Libertarian) observers inside the polling places. Even when pro-Trump (2020) and pro-Lake (2022) mobs surrounded the voting Center in Phoenix, Arizona, and demanded entrance, Republican observers watched the counting.

Lie

4. After it became clear that then-President Trump was losing in 2020, he and his team claimed that the voting machines were programmed to switch votes from Trump to Biden.

    Perhaps Trump and his allies thought that if they cast enough doubt, something would turn up that would show the machines were, in fact, programmed or manipulated against then-President Trump. They promoted so many falsehoods, that they succeeded in planting doubt among millions of decent Americans about the quality of our electoral system. That doubt led to a reliance on the lies of one self-styled strongman—Mr. Trump.

    Some people may have believed these fantastic allegations, but they were, in fact, out-and-out, oft-repeated lies. What was the intent? Look at the results. The effect is to challenge, weaken, and destroy the rule of law.

True

Then-President Trump's own team at the Department of Homeland Security and its Cybersecurity and Infrastructure Security Agency coordinated the machinery testing of the 2020 election. The truth is that, especially in Maricopa County, Arizona, the Dominion Democracy machines used in the 2020 elections were among the best in the country. They had been independently certified multiple times before the Election, and through numerous post-election audits for accuracy, with no vote switching having occurred.

The 2020 election used more paper ballots and verified them more successfully than ever before. Perhaps you recall the fiasco of the "dangling chads" in the 2000 Florida election, which involved digital voting? In Arizona in 2020, everyone cast their ballots on paper.

According to Major Garrett and David Becker, all the Trump team's lies about the election of 2020 were not random or haphazard. They were part of a conscious plan to overturn the election. "The most chilling example of this is the revelation of the draft Trump executive order… that sought to enlist the Department of Defense and Homeland Security to seize voting machines—presumably as an excuse to keep Trump indefinitely and unconstitutionally in power."[104]

CHAPTER 27

THREATS, LIES, TRUTHS— 2022 TO THE PRESENT

2022
Lies

In November 2022, former news anchor and Trump-endorsed Kari Lake was running for Governor of Arizona against Democrat Katie Hobbs. Kari Lake—always dressed impeccably—lied continually during and after the election. She lied about signatures on mail-in ballots not matching those on file. False. She lied about intentionally misprinted ballots rejected in Republican areas. False. She claimed "hundreds of thousands of ballots" were mishandled. False. She claimed that people had snuck fake ballots into batches before officials counted them. False. Even after she lost the election to Katie Hobbs (it was close, but clear), she lied: "I am the duly elected governor. They just stole it." False.

Lake sued Hobbs in Arizona and federal court claiming she, Lake, had won the election.[105] She lost every lawsuit.

Lies and Threats

Ms. Lake also made false defamatory statements against Supervisor Bill Gates and Stephen Richer, the then (2022) duly-elected County Recorder. Her lies incited harassment and even death threats to Mr. Richer and his family. She told supporters that Richer and Gates "sabotaged Election Day," falsely accusing them of deliberately "printing the wrong image on ballots to jam tabulators and injecting hundreds of thousands of phone ballots."[106]

Mr. Gates ultimately had to defend the election process against such false allegations in 16 separate press conferences during the days leading up to and following the November 2022 election. He and his family faced serious threats. Bill's wife packed their bags and she and their daughters fled their home for an undisclosed safe house.[107]

The Supervisors were not the only ones under threat. While still County Recorder in 2020, Adrian Fontes began hiring personal security agents, and the County provided Secretary of State employees with hotel rooms or accommodations at locations other than their homes.[108] Newly elected County Recorder Stephen Richer also faced numerous threats and accusations.

Meanwhile, on election night, November 2022, Supervisor Gates was sequestered at the vote-counting center. Drones and a helicopter flew the skies, and police on horseback patrolled the roads around the center. Crowds of angry pro-Trump and pro-Lake demonstrators demanded entrance to MCTEC to control the vote. It felt like a war zone.[109]

True

Maricopa County experienced some issues with its printers (not the Dominion tabulators) in the 2022 elections. The Maricopa County Republican Party censured Chairman Bill Gates and all five of the Supervisors due to claims of "avoidable errors" that led to "significant voter disenfranchisement."[110]

However, an external investigation—not conducted by the County *or* the Republican Party—found that those problems were due to equipment failure, not intentional misconduct, and did not affect the outcome of the election or the ability of voters who actually wanted to cast their votes.[111]

Lies and Threats

In the autumn of 2022, Kari Lake sued Governor Katie Hobbs, claiming she had won the election when, in fact, she had lost.

After the 2022 election, Ms. Lake falsely accused County Recorder Stephen Richer and County Supervisor Bill Gates of sabotaging Election Day by deliberately printing the wrong image on ballots to jam tabulators and getting hundreds of thousands of phony ballots. As a direct result of Lake's lies, followers of Trump and Lake insulted both Gates and Richer as to the integrity of their work and threatened their lives and the lives of their families.[112]

2025
Lies and Threats

Meanwhile, on June 20, 2025, the now President Trump tweeted—again, after five years—that they should appoint a special prosecutor to investigate the 2020 elections. After all the election workers, after all the Court evaluations, after all the certifications and extra investigations—both certifiably independent and certifiably biased for Trump—after all the audits proved the validity and accuracy of the election results, one man trumpeted suggestions of going after people for a "crime."[113]

After returning to the presidency in early 2025, Mr. Trump pardoned all individuals (after convictions in various courts of law) who had illegally attempted to halt the Constitutional transfer of power in 2020 to incoming President Biden. Mr. Trump then directed his Department of Justice to investigate Chris Krebs, a former Trump cybersecurity appointee who had vouched for the security and accuracy of the 2020 elections.[114]

Early in 2025, as a trial date approached in one of the Dominion cases, President Trump issued an executive order attacking the law firm that had litigated on behalf of Dominion in the Fox case. A federal judge handling that case said the framers [of the Constitution] would view his attack as "a shocking abuse of power."[115]

On August 14, 2025, continuing his false narrative, Mr. Trump posted on his Trump Social.

> "Social media has again condemned mail-in ballots"— even though they have been proven time and again to be even more accurate and secure.
>
> "I am going to lead a movement to get rid of MAIL-IN BALLOTS, and also, while we're at it, Highly 'Inaccurate,' Very Expensive, and Seriously Controversial VOTING MACHINES.
>
> "Remember, the states are merely an 'agent' for the Federal Government in counting and tabulating the votes. They must do what the Federal Government, as represented by the President of the United States, tells them, FOR THE GOOD OF OUR COUNTRY, to do."[116]

True

Mail-in ballots are popular among Republicans and Democrats, and are necessary for our men and women in uniform serving overseas. Election officials double-check them (more than in-person votes) to confirm voter accuracy. The States, according to our Constitution, control tabulations. The President does not. Mr. Trump is again lying and again urging conduct that violates the laws of our country.

We kid you not.

Challenging What Works

On August 20, 2025, the Free Enterprise Club argued in the Arizona Court of Appeals that the state's method for verifying signatures over the past four years violates state law.

This case has been going on for a few years. However, a change to the *Election Procedure Manual (EPM)* in 2023 expanded what was acceptable for comparing signatures. The 2023 *EPM* advised using ballot affidavits and poll book signatures. This change was codified into Arizona law. The judge emphasized that the new statutes used the *EPM* phrase "registration record," and did not eliminate "prior early ballot affidavits" as a comparison tool.

Although the Free Enterprise Club has claimed that using signatures from a voter's ballot affidavit or poll books in a previous election "would open up the possibility of increased voter fraud," no fraud—through several election seasons—has been found.[117]

This case regarding voter signature verification is of particular interest since a group of us took a tour of the MCTEC on August 20, 2025—the same day as the Court of Appeals heard the arguments. The tour guide, a decade-long veteran of the County Recorder's Office, spent almost half an hour showing us how officials compare voter signatures, including the use of prior signatures on mail-in ballot envelopes. The tour guide emphasized the specialized training of all those who work on signature verification, highlighting the specific points in a signature that provide clues to accuracy or lack thereof. She then clarified that if there is a question, MCTEC specialists contact the voter in person to verify the accuracy of the signatures (or lack thereof). None of the experts wants fraud, and none of the experts allows fraud.

It appears that the Free Enterprise Club intends to reduce the number of voter-provided signatures for comparison purposes, thereby increasing the likelihood of proving more voter fraud and potentially reducing the number of voters. Free Enterprise might serve itself better—if voter fraud detection and elimination is the real goal— by taking the tour and even becoming trained as specialists in voter signature comparison.

Meanwhile, Justin Heap—a denier of the valid 2020 election results—defeated Stephen Richer in the 2024 Republican primary for the position of County Recorder. In 2025, he sued the Board of Supervisors to obtain more control over the election process, which the 2019 Board and Recorder had successfully negotiated to return specific statutory authority to the BOS.

Before taking office in January 2025, Heap had called the County elections a "laughingstock," despite the numerous checks, investigations, and audits that have shown the Maricopa County elections process to be one of the best in the country. It also put Heap at odds with Thomas Galvin, an incoming Republican Supervisor who has defended the county's elections.

It turns out that Mr. Heap privately tried to pressure several members of the BOS to support him in his effort to get more control. Initially, he failed to properly maintain key public records related to his oversight of the elections. So, his record was not promising for improving the election system.

Votebeat, a nonprofit news organization, sued for records of his phone texts with officials on the Board of Supervisors under the Arizona Public Records Law. At first, Heap denied having records (following a July 1 letter from the BOS's County Attorney requesting fulfillment of the records), then claimed his phone had been damaged. When *Votebeat* received records from Supervisor Debbie Lesko that included a text from Heap, it became clear that Heap was withholding public records. Heap then obtained a private criminal defense lawyer, Barry Mitchell, rather than the County Attorney. Finally, Mitchell sent copies of about 135 texts to *Votebeat.*

The texts showed that Heap had tried to pressure Lesko and fellow Supervisor Mark Stewart to go around Chairman Thomas Galvin during the negotiations.

Among other things, after being denied support by Lesko and Stewart, Heap claimed that he had obtained support from the sole Democratic Supervisor, Steve Gallardo. Gallardo has vigorously stated that Heap is lying. Gallardo has no reason to support Heap. The BOS has overseen elections competently in 2020, 2022, and 2024. Gallardo has asked the Arizona Attorney General to investigate

Heap on suspicion of public corruption, based on his claims in the texts.[118]

It seems evident that the challenges to election integrity continue. From the outset, those who were unjustly attacked began to respond.

CHAPTER 28

STRIKING BACK

2021

In March 2021, Dominion Voting Systems filed a defamation lawsuit against Fox News. Dominion focused on allegations made between November 2020 and January 2021. Documents in the case indicate that the prominent hosts and top executives of Fox were aware that Fox was reporting false statements and continued to do so to retain viewers for financial reasons. On April 18, 2023, the parties settled. Fox agreed to pay Dominion $787.5 million and also acknowledged that Fox had broadcast false statements about Dominion.[119]

On May 17, 2021, all members of the Maricopa County BOS, plus Stephen Richer, Maricopa County Recorder, and Paul Penzone, Maricopa County Sheriff, sent an email letter to Senate President Karen Fann in response to her May 12 letter and Tweet accusing the County of "deleting a directory full of databases from the 2020 election system days before the election equipment was delivered to the audit."

The e-letter specified the following:

1. **Your accusation that Maricopa County deleted data is false.** That the Senate would launch such a grave accusation via Twitter not only before waiting for an answer to your questions, but also before your so-called "audit" [is complete] demonstrates to the world that the Arizona Senate is not acting in good faith...but is only interested in feeding the various festering conspiracy theories

that fuel the fundraising schemes of those pulling your strings…The… Arizona Senate is held up to ridicule in every corner of the globe, and our democracy is imperiled.

2. **Your various questions about our election procedures reveal a serious lack of understanding of election law, as well as the best practices utilized by Maricopa County and other jurisdictions for the conduct of elections.**

3. **We cannot produce what we do not possess; and, we do not possess additional passwords.**

4. **We will not provide your "auditors" access to the County's routers because doing so would compromise the security of the County's network, which in turn could compromise the security of sensitive, protected and critical data.**

5. **We will not attend your meeting on May 18, 2021.**

6. **Your "audit" is harming all of us, and we ask you to end it.**

   You are photographing ballots contrary to the laws that the Senate helped enact, and you are sending those images to unidentified places and people…

   You certainly must recognize that things are not going well at the Coliseum [the location of the Cyber Ninja activity].

   Unfortunately, this has become a partisan issue, and it should not be one. It is time to make a choice to defend the Constitution and the Republic. As County elected officials, we come from different political parties, but we stand united together to defend the Constitution and the Republic in our opposition to the Big Lie. We ask everyone to join us in standing for the truth. The

November 3, 2020, general election was free and fair and conducted by the Elections Department with integrity and honor...

It is time to end this. For the good of the Senate, for the good of the Country, and for the good of the Democratic institutions that define us as American.[120]

On June 25, 2021, the U.S. Deputy Attorney General issued a Memorandum for all Federal Prosecutors and the Director of the FBI. It was an attempt to prevent and reduce the increased violence against election workers.

The subject was "Guidance Regarding Threats Against Election Workers." The Deputy Attorney General said,

In recent months, there has been a significant increase in the threat of violence against Americans who administer free and fair elections throughout our Nation...There are many things that are open to debate in America. But the right of all eligible citizens to vote is not one of them...

For this vital right to be effective, election officials must be permitted to do their jobs free from improper partisan influence, physical threats, and any other conduct designed to intimidate...

To assist with this important effort, the Department is launching a task force—including members from the Criminal Division, the Civil Rights Division, the National Security Division and the FBI—to address the rise in threats against election officials.[121]

On August 11, 2021, Dominion filed a defamation lawsuit against Trump attorney Sidney Powell, et al, Rudolph W. Giuliani, and MY PILLOW, INC. et al. in the Washington, D.C. Federal District Court.

2022

In January 2022, the Maricopa County Elections Department and the Office of the Recorder sent a 93-page document to the Arizona Senate, called "Correcting the Record." It was an in-depth, precise, fully documented and thorough analysis of the false and/or misleading claims and the faulty or inaccurate conclusions in the Cyber Ninja Report. As a sample, CYFir (one of the Senate's contractors) "did not make a single accurate claim" ... and "The Senate did not subpoena the archived files." What the Senate subpoenaed was delivered to the Veteran's Coliseum on April 21 and 22, 2021, and, as signed off by the Senate, the County was in "full compliance" with the subpoena.[122]

In December 2022, a U.S. District Court judge sanctioned Ms. Lake for making "false, misleading, and unsupported factual assertions." Lies. After losing her election bid for Arizona governor, Kari Lake sued Governor Katie Hobbs, claiming she won the election when in fact she had lost. The federal judge, who dismissed her case, stated that she was "furthering false narratives that baselessly undermine public trust. You were sanctioned for lying to the court."[123]

2023

Again, in May 2023, the Arizona Supreme Court sanctioned Ms. Lake for "making false factual statements."[124]

In June 2023, the case of *Arizona vs Stuart Hadland* was filed in Pima County against the man who threatened to poison Bill Gates multiple times so that he would die. Hadland was found guilty. On January 31, 2024, the Court sentenced Hadland to three years of probation, no contact with Mr. Gates or his family, and mandatory mental health services. Gates thanked prosecutors and law enforcement, saying,

"As a society, we should neither normalize nor tolerate threats of violence against one another." Attorney General Kris Mays said she would continue to prosecute "those who seek to undermine our democracy through intimidation and violence."[125]

On June 28, 2023, to protect their employee, Elections Director Scott Jarrett, the Maricopa County BOS unanimously reappointed him to his position—and assigned him to a new boss. She was Jen Pokorski, the County Manager, appointed in April 2023. Supervisor Jack Sellers emphasized, "Elected officials [such as the Supervisors and County Recorder] should not have a direct report handling elections. And this gets us to that point."[126]

Jen Pokorski served at the pleasure of the BOS, but they could not directly hire or fire other county staff. Therefore, if a future [elected] Board wanted to remove a department head under Pokorski's domain, such as Jarrett, she would have to agree to fire him. This vote was intended to insulate Jarrett, or someone in his position, from contentious politics. "Scott Jarrett is in an extremely tough and visible position. This is just the ability to tell our people who work for this county, we stand behind you," said Chairman Clint Hickman.[127]

Also, in June 2023, Stephen Richer, whose entire family had received threats, sued Kari Lake for defamation. He knew he had run a clean, efficient, secure, and transparent election. Richer also sought damages to reimburse him and his wife for the thousands of dollars he said they had spent to install new security features in their home after, he said, Lake's false statements spurred threats of violence and harassment.[128] He also asked for an award of punitive damages, compensation for damage to his reputation and mental health, and for Ms. Lake to admit that her claims about him were false.[129]

On Tuesday, March 23, 2024, Ms. Lake indicated she would not contest Richer's claims that she had lied and defamed him. Richer said her claims turned his life and that of his family "upside down" and made them "the targets of threats of violence, even death."[130]

Ultimately, Ms. Lake and Mr. Richer entered a confidential settlement agreement rather than going to trial. The matter was "resolved to the satisfaction of both parties."[131]

In August 2023, an intensely emotional trial occurred in which an Iowa man had threatened the lives of both Supervisor Clint Hickman and Attorney General Mark Brnovich. They had been victims of the same Iowa phone caller. The U.S. District Attorney brought federal charges for interstate threats. Other persons who had been supervisors or fellow-victims of threats sat in the Courtroom for support. Among them were Bill Gates and Andy Kunasek, former County Supervisor, and County Recorder Stephen Richer and his wife.[132]

Mr. Hickman requested leniency. Most of Hickman's supporters had tears in their eyes as he spoke to the judge. But the judge stated that multiple death threats crossed the line and sentenced the defendant, Mr. Mark Rissi, to over two years in a federal prison.

Kris Mays had been elected Attorney General in January 2023. In March 2023, she confirmed the existence of an investigation of the "fake elector" case in Arizona, in which 11 Republicans had created fake documents declaring themselves the real "electors"—to cast their votes for Mr. Trump—even though they knew Biden was the duly elected President-to-be. Georgia, Michigan, and Nevada had already begun investigations of similar "fake" elector slates. Arizona was the fourth state to investigate the illegal efforts to overturn the election through a "fake" elector slate.[133]

On April 25, 2024, an Arizona Grand Jury in Maricopa County handed up a 58-page indictment against 11 Arizona Republicans and seven top Trump aides. The case is famously known as *State of Arizona v. Kelli Ward, et al.* Each defendant charged with numerous felony counts.

The felony counts included:

- Conspiracy
- Fraudulent Schemes and Artifices for knowingly benefitting from fraud designed to prevent the lawful transfer of the presidency against the will of Arizona voters
- Fraudulent Schemes and Practices by concealing facts or making false statements filed by the Arizona Republican electors
- Forgery (six counts) for each Trump/Pence certificate filed with the Vice President of the U.S.; two with the Arizona Secretary of State, two with the Archivist of the U.S., and one with the Chief Judge of the federal District Court for the District of Arizona.

The Arizona fake electors were: Tyler Bowyer, Nancy Cottle, Jake Hoffman, Anthony Kern, Jim Lamon, Robert Montgomery, Samuel Moorhead, Loraine Pellegrino, Greg Safsten, Kelli Ward, and her husband, Michael Ward.

The un-indicted co-conspirators were: Donald Trump, Kelly Townsend, Mark Finchem, Kenneth Chesebro, and Jack Wilenchik.

Both Andy Biggs and Paul Gosar, two Trump-allied Arizona congressmen who attempted to subvert the Arizona election, received subpoenas because of their connection to this matter.[134]

In October 2023, Kenneth Chesebro, a Trump ally, pleaded guilty in the Georgia prosecutions. Arizona investigators had interviewed him in 2022, and he had provided information that allowed Attorney General Mays to target Trump allies from out of state who participated in the Arizona fake elector scheme.

However, as of the summer of 2025, this case remained stalled in court proceedings. The judge ruled that the prosecution failed to inform the Grand Jury about the federal Electoral Count Act.[135]

2025

The reminders of repeated lies by pro-Trump actors—and the need to strike back—continued. On June 25, 2025, Arizona Representative Greg Stanton took Kari Lake to task during a Congressional House Foreign Affairs Committee hearing. She had lost in Arizona in a governor's race in 2022, a U.S. Senate race in 2024, and lied "shamelessly" about her own elections.

Ms. Lake was appointed in 2025 by re-elected President Trump to serve as Senior Advisor for the U.S. Agency for Global Media. Regarding her actions to dismantle Voice of America, Stanton said,

> Ms. Lake, we shouldn't be dismantling the agency that combats propaganda from the Chinese Communist Party, the Kremlin and Tehran…. Your job is to tell the people of the world the truth about America. Because of that, there's a…fundamental issue I want to address today: Character…I've seen you in action, including your behavior in the last two elections [in Arizona] … You lost [the 2022 election] fair and square. Instead of conceding, you embarrassed yourself and our state by lying—again and again—blaming everything under the sun for your loss except your own toxic politics. You lie about that election to this day.[136]

On August 18, 2025, Dominion Voting Systems won a settlement against the right-wing show, Newsmax, for $67 million for defamation. It is one of several lawsuits brought by Dominion against various news media outlets that alleged Dominion's election "rigging" for Biden in 2020. There is evidence in virtually all cases that the individuals within their respective news media were lying, and they communicated within the organizations that they knew they were lying. Internal correspondence from Newsmax officials revealed that they were aware their claims against Dominion were baseless. Several court cases remain unsettled.[137]

Another lawsuit from another voting machine manufacturer, Smartmatic—also a target of pro-Trump conspiracy theories—was settled with Fox News for $40 million. The judge found that it was "CRYSTAL clear" that none of Fox's allegations about Smartmatic were true.[138]

As attacks on truth and democratic institutions persist, there will undoubtedly be further efforts to counter them. In their own words, the six upheld their integrity by speaking truth to power.

CHAPTER 29

SPEAKING TRUTH TO POWER

The six who stopped the steal conducted themselves with integrity throughout the 2020 election season and afterward. Together, with all the men and women working to carry out a fair election, they made their case from the start.

As the November 3, 2020 election came to a close, the BOS acknowledged that the majority of votes went to Joe Biden and that there were threats and pressure from outsiders to alter the results.

On November 4, Clint Hickman and Steve Gallardo, in an effort to demonstrate bipartisan understanding of and support for the election process, sent a letter to all constituents and political actors. They appealed to reason.

Dear Maricopa County voters,

As members of the Maricopa County Board of Supervisors, we are concerned about the misinformation spreading about the integrity of our elections.

First, vote counting is not a Republican or Democrat issue; everyone should want all the votes to be counted, whether they were mailed or cast in person. An accurate vote takes time. It's possible the results you see now may change after all the votes are counted. This is evidence of democracy, not fraud.

Second, Sharpies do not invalidate ballots. We did extensive testing on multiple different types of ink with our new vote tabulation equipment. Sharpies are recommended by the manufacturer because they provide the fastest-drying ink. Our Elections Department has been communicating this publicly for several weeks.

Maricopa County has bipartisan oversight of elections in 2020 with the Board of Supervisors and the Recorder's Office each playing an important role. We would like to thank the hundreds of volunteers, poll workers and staff for being a part of an incredible Elections team. All of us are committed to a fair and efficient count of all votes.

Thank you,
Clint Hickman, Chairman,
Maricopa County Board of Supervisors
Steve Gallardo, Supervisor, District 5,
Maricopa County Board of Supervisors[139]

Scott Jarrett and Rey Valenzuela, co-directors of the Elections Department, conducted a post-election audit in the weeks immediately following Election Day. They presented their extensive report to the Board of Supervisors on November 20, 2020. Having spent considerable time following the audit and Logic and Analysis process, Hickman knew the results of the presidential election clearly showed that Joe Biden was the winner. As Chairman of the BOS, he recognized that his leadership and integrity were crucial. On November 17 (see Chapter 22), he circulated a letter to the Board and to Maricopa County constituents expressing his beliefs and concerns about the election results and the responsibility of the BOS. He made it clear that he would vote to certify the election results.

Rusty Bowers, Speaker of the Arizona House of Representatives, who also faced pressure, had already made himself clear to the Supervisors. In a letter to the BOS, which Chairman Clint Hickman read to the full committee on November 20, 2020—at the BOS Certification Hearing—Bowers said:

> I am not going to violate the law or deviate from my own moral compass, as some have pushed me to do and some have probably pushed others to do.

Hickman concluded:

> I appreciate the efforts of our elections staff who worked tirelessly to run this election during a pandemic. No matter how you voted, this election was administered with integrity, transparency, and, most importantly, in accordance with Arizona state laws.[140]

After the two-and-a-half-hour Certification Hearing in November, having asked every relevant question they could think of and being satisfied with the answers, all five Supervisors made statements honoring the work of the elections staff and workers. They voted unanimously to certify the election results.

In January 2021, at virtually the same time as Mr. Trump told followers to march to the Capitol, and when rioters broke into the building and attempted to prevent the peaceful transfer of power, Bowers resisted pressure to call a special session of the legislature to rescind the popular vote of the people. However, according to the Arizona Constitution, a special session can only be called by the Governor on their own or upon receipt of a petition signed by two-thirds of the legislators from both chambers. House Speaker Bowers knew it was not within his legal or Constitutional authority. By his refusal, Bowers spoke a greater truth than words alone.

In February, Arizona Senator Paul Boyer faced immense pressure to vote with all Republicans to hold all five Supervisors in contempt and have them jailed for failing to deliver documents demanded by the Arizona Senate.

The Supervisors had sued in Maricopa County Superior Court to ask the Court to clarify the law. The law for which they sought Court clarification—A.R.S. § 16-624. A & B & D—said:

> A. After the canvass has been completed, the officer in charge of elections shall deposit the package or envelope containing the ballots in a secure facility managed by the county treasurer, who shall keep it unopened and unaltered for twenty-four months for elections for a federal office...
>
> B. Irregular ballots shall be preserved for six months after the election and the packages containing them may be opened and the contents examined only upon an order of the court...
>
> C. If a recount is ordered or a contest begun within six months, the county treasurer may be ordered by the court... and thereupon they shall be in the custody and control of the court.

The Arizona statute referred to a court order. It did not mention a legislative subpoena. The Supervisors believed they were honoring the Constitution and democracy. The BOS employed the peaceful, time-honored approach of allowing the Court to settle the matter of interpreting the law.

On February 8, Boyer was the only Republican to vote "no" to the resolution for contempt, thus defeating the Republican effort. In addressing the Senate, Boyer asked for cooperation between the Senate and the Supervisors:

> I've always said so long as there's hope for both sides to work with one another, I want to do all I can in

my limited power to have us work amicably together. We still have time to work together on this.

My no vote today will give the Board time to resolve itself on how to legally proceed with providing these public records for independent sunshine and scrutiny, while also providing 100% protection for the private nature of an individual's vote. This is Arizona; we know how to walk and chew gum at the same time.

I've heard from both sides, and there has been some mistrust of the other side's respective motives, whether it's been due to media interviews, press releases, or social media posts. Which is why it's critical that we, the State Senate and the County Board of Supervisors, find a way to amicably work together and address the concerns of both sides.

No elected office, whether at the County Board level or the state legislative level, should have to have a police presence outside of their homes due to a sincere policy disagreement (Speaker Bowers, some of the BOS members).

I believe the Board genuinely seeks the confidence and clarity from a Court order to legally proceed. They seek to obtain it, and we seek that they get that legal confidence post haste.

Overall, I believe the Maricopa County Board of Supervisors has no policy disagreement with additional audits of the last election, and ultimately that is exactly what should happen. An abundance of oversight and review of government is precisely the job of this Senate. It will happen where all parties have legal confidence, it should happen without contempt charges, and the legal process to proceed is underway.

Arizona citizens demand confidence, clarity, and TRANSPARENCY in their election system. Audits provide more confidence, more sunshine.

The Arizona Senate demands that those voter expectations are met, and it is my opinion that the subpoena power is clearly both a broad and effective tool to provide accountability to our citizens. It is used sparingly, and reluctantly for an important reason. **Measured restraint is a virtue.**

Subpoenas to legislative committees are about providing a public, transparent conversation in front of our citizens. That authority is clear, and it WILL be used if necessary.

Lawmakers should be praised, not condemned, for passionately protecting the will of the voters. It's noble, and it's righteous.

Make no mistake, today's vote merely provides a little bit more time for us to work together charitably and amicably as friends for the sole purpose of gaining more clarity. It is NOT a final determination, nor is it the end of this process.

My vote today is about prayerful patience. It's about resolving disagreements civilly, and these are things that I believe all of the Senators can agree upon, regardless of our respective vote today.[141]

In March 2021, the Court resolved the matter in favor of the Senate, holding that the Senate had the power to subpoena documents. The Court also emphasized the Senate's obligation to maintain confidentiality for specific documents, particularly voter information. The BOS cooperated, and the Senate proceeded with its audit of the 2020 General Election, also known as the Cyber Ninja Audit. When the BOS delivered the subpoenaed documents to the

Veterans' Coliseum in March, 2021, the Senate confirmed that the BOS had fully complied with their subpoena.

In June 2022, the U.S. House of Representatives Oversight Committee held hearings on the January 6, 2021, riots at the Capitol. Rusty Bowers testified about the inappropriate pressure that had been put upon him by then-President Trump and his lawyer, Rudy Giuliani. Bowers noted that Trump was clever not to be directly involved in the phone calls, but had told Bowers that Giuliani could work with him.

Giuliani pushed allegations of fraudulent voting by undocumented immigrants or dead people. When Bowers insisted upon evidence, Giuliani said, "We have lots of theories, we just don't have the evidence." Bowers also stated that Giuliani pressured him in December 2020 to call the Arizona legislature back into session to recall the electors that would be going to President Biden after Biden beat Trump in Arizona—a unilateral move that Bowers said he could not legally do. That move would be unconstitutional.

"It is a tenet of my faith that the Constitution is divinely inspired," said Bowers. "I would not do it." Mr. Bowers said that Mr. Trump had asked him to hold a hearing to investigate allegations, but he thought the evidence did not merit a hearing. "You are asking me to do something against my oath, and I will not break my oath," he told Trump and Giuliani.

Giuliani responded, "Aren't we all Republicans here? I would think we'd get a better reception."

Trump lawyer John Eastman also pressured Bowers, asking him to set up a vote in the legislature to decertify the electors for Arizona. Bowers noted,

> "His suggestion was that we would do it, and
> I said I can't," adding that Eastman told him to just
> do it and let the courts sort it out. "But who are these
> people that they would do this to America? Is this what

civil discourse means nowadays? Have we gotten so bad that we have to act this way?"

He concluded, "I'm against bullying and emotional violence against anybody, especially over the sacredness of our vote."[142]

On October 7, 2021, the U.S. House Oversight Committee held more hearings—this time on the 2020 elections and the Arizona audit. Jack Sellers, who was at that time the Chairman of the Maricopa County Board of Supervisors, testified:

> I want to start by saying that the election on November 3, 2020, in Maricopa County was free, fair, and accurate. I sit before you today as a Republican who was voted into office in November 2020…
>
> But the most important people involved in the November election were the men and women of the Maricopa County Elections Department. They executed a secure, accurate, and efficient election of over 1.8 million voters in the Nation's fourth most populous county during a worldwide pandemic. Our Election Department was praised by election experts throughout the country, and we received an award from the National Association of Counties.
>
> Maricopa County began planning for the 2020 election immediately after the November 2018 election results were canvassed and submitted to the Arizona Secretary of State… We also knew that the election results in Maricopa County would play a pivotal role in both the outcome of the Presidential race and the U.S. Senate chamber political makeup.
>
> I'm very proud of the efforts we put forth to prepare. We worked closely with the Arizona Secretary of State, our legislative leaders in both the Arizona

House and the Senate, the Attorney General, and the Governor's office.

We were also very inclusive of all the political parties who participated fully in not only observing Election Day administration and tabulation, but also in pre- and post-election Logic and Accuracy testing. If you were in Arizona politics in November 2020 and didn't understand how Maricopa County was running elections, then you just weren't paying attention.

The county invested in a very robust voter education campaign.

We implemented the technology to educate our residents on …when and how to register, how you can vote, where you can vote, and the wait times at the polling stations, all by pushing a button on your phone.

We ran a Presidential preference election in February [March]. All participants agreed it was well-run and accurate.

We ran a primary election in August 2020. Again, the public, the candidates, and the political parties all agreed that the managing of the election by the County was excellent.

We ran the 2020 general election in November, and suddenly, what to that point had been a great process was deemed to be fatally flawed by a small, yet loud minority.

It was not a flawed election process, not a lack of security. It was a candidate that many Maricopa County Republicans simply did not support.

I was naive in thinking that I could just sit down with our State Senate leadership and explain the answers to their questions and accusations, and we could put this uncertainty behind us and move on with securing a fruitful future for our residents. But it's become clear that there are those who don't care what the facts are. They just want to gain political power and raise money by fostering mistrust of the greatest power an individual can exercise in the United States, which is their vote.[143]

Next, Bill Gates testified:

> Madame Chair, Ranking Member, thank you for having me here today to discuss a topic of great importance: the future of free and fair elections in the greatest country in the world.
>
> The 2020 general election in Maricopa County, Arizona, was the best election we have run to date. I can say that because it has also been the most scrutinized. Election professionals have said it. Hand counts and machine tests have affirmed it. Courts have reaffirmed it…Ninety percent of voters were very satisfied…
>
> By all measures, our election was run securely, and everyone who wanted to participate could.
>
> But that is not what you hear from some members of my party. Instead, they have denigrated the good work done by our elections team and fanned the flames of conspiracy. This willingness to actively promote or quietly appease those peddling claims of election fraud resulted in the first non-peaceful transfer of power in our history.
>
> Somehow, election integrity has become a never-ending series of questions, designed to cast doubt, not restore trust. To these folks, widespread fraud is assumed as a reason for any political loss. Facts to the contrary are ignored.

Even though more Arizonans chose Joe Biden as their President, 20 Arizona legislators signed a resolution last December [2020], attempting to get Congress to accept 11 alternate electoral votes for Donald J. Trump…a staggering act of defiance of the people's will.

State senators went to court to get the people's ballots and federally-certified election equipment, quote "sufficiently in advance of the congressional review of the Electoral College returns on January 6, 2021."

When that failed, senators carried on…threatening to jail members of our Board…and casting doubt on the results of the two independent, professional audits we authorized…which found no evidence of vote switching or hacking and no issue with election equipment or software.

It should have ended there. It did not…

I have been a member of the Maricopa County Board of Supervisors for four years. In that time, we have taken significant steps to help people vote when and how they want. We have developed new processes and organizational structures to ensure accountability and security.

Election integrity is not a new issue for me; as a former election attorney for the Arizona Republican Party, it is a passion of mine. That's why I'm here to tell you that what is happening across our country right now—the disinformation campaigns and calls to decertify fair elections—these efforts are the most serious threat to American democracy I have seen so far in my lifetime.

If elected officials don't put truth above party, private-funded, government-backed inquiries into legitimate elections will continue. Supporters of losing candidates will find financial backers to help them challenge the results. Trust in our democratic process will plummet.

Madame Chair and members, as a Republican who believes in democracy, I have dreamed of someday assisting a nation where democracy is taking hold. Perhaps a former Soviet Republic like Tajikistan or Belarus. I never thought I would have to do this same work in my home country, here in the United States of America. Thank you.[144]

After the November 2022, interim elections, the Maricopa County BOS conducted an independent review and audit. There had been some malfunctioning of older printing machines [not the Dominion Democracy 5.B tabulation machines]. They hired retired Arizona Judge Ruth McGregor to conduct the investigation.

On April 10, 2023, the Board of Supervisors (BOS) reported that the investigation was complete. BOS Chairman Clint Hickman said,

> I pushed for an outside investigation as soon as this happened, and I appreciate Justice McGregor and her team's thorough, professional, and independent review. We don't grade our own homework, and now that we have a better idea of the factors involved, we'll make changes to best serve voters, starting with replacing some equipment.[145]

On August 28, 2023, at the sentencing hearing in the trial against Iowan Mark Rissi for interstate death threats, Hickman spoke in open court to the defendant, the judge, and all those present. He addressed the years of threats and attacks, the support of friends, and a request for leniency:

There's a lot of things going through my head over the many years of attacks. I don't know if these threats were made because I'm a politician sporting the Republican symbol. I don't know if I'm being attacked because I'm a husband, a father, or a Little League baseball coach.

In the front row are three gentlemen who have had death threats placed against them that either have current cases or cases that have been sentenced. That man, Andy, witnessed a supervisor being shot in our auditorium with real bullets.

This case is about the bullets that are words.

My family has lived through almost a nightmare with my public service…I did ask [my wife] what would you like the court to know. She said, "I trust whatever you're going to say. We've been through it. How about this, we'd like it to stop. I'm fatigued."

Okay. So that is basically where a lot of us are finding ourselves in with public service, we are fatigued with these attacks.

But I'm certainly supported by my County family back here that have the audacity to do a job out there transparently running elections. They are great people…

So hopefully Mr. Rissi and his family will walk a little bit in my shoes during this time.

During this time when I was chairman and trying to canvass an election and finally getting it canvassed, that was the most stress I had ever as a chairman because I had to bring this vote up to a canvass to some of my peers…not knowing if they had their questions answered, not knowing if they did the research to find out if they truly believe Maricopa County ran a fair, transparent, and just election. I sat on pins and needles that night [November 19, 2020], wondering if we were going to canvass an election because of all the craziness that was going on and the threats. I wouldn't have blamed any of them for standing down. I wouldn't have blamed any of them for not even showing up to do their job, but they did. And all five of us made great statements. And we have been a team.

But on a night in December [2020], ninety people came [to the Hickman home]. A person called me and said, "Tonight, Clint, they're coming to your house…" I called Sheriff Penzone. He said, "Well, we'll put a couple of guys out there."

I was standing with these two protection officers in front of my house when the undercover investigator said, he's not lying, there are a hundred people and they just announced they're coming to Clint's house.

They told me, "Clint, you need to stay in your house. You need to get your family and you need to stay in your house."

I said, "No. I'm going to face this head-on."

He said, "Hey, let us do our jobs as law enforcement officers. Not only do we want you to stay in that house, we are going to tell them you're not there. You can't move a curtain."

So, you guys feel what that's like to tell your family, your teenage boys, we need to stay here. There are people coming to our home, and you need to sit here and be quiet and listen to this. You may think that didn't show strength.

But it did. Mr. Rissi, you gave…me the greatest gift because my boys and my family got to see me operate as a strong leader with character and conviction and passion for this job. Because I told my boys, "We're going to stay here and we're going to listen. But if there's a door pounding, we're going to go out there and we're going to help those officers because they're going to need it." So they were prepared, and they knew.

They got to see me stand up to that.

I love that I have my family's support. And, Mr. Rissi, I see some people in the audience, and I bet— you touched on it—you probably had some similar frightening times.

Those times didn't put fear in my heart. This put strength in my heart.

But you probably had some fear when the FBI visited you. Your family probably had fear. So they're going to need your support.

I appreciate that you have come here to make amends. I appreciate that you have decided to plead guilty so you don't put my family through the court to talk about this again.

And I really hope you, Judge Lanza… you are justice incarnate in this room…I know you're going to make the right decision…But if you wanted to know my vote, I would expect we are never going to… change this if we don't start looking at this like this year is about grace, humility, and charity…I think that you will show this man grace and humility and charity. I know that you have to perform a job when it comes to sentencing, but I ask you to be extremely gracious with your wisdom and show this man compassion—to show that we all put our hand on that Bible and it's about love. So hopefully you will show God's grace and love to this man as you sentence him.…

> I've had a long life and I do not think I've ever
> had it in my mind… to make a death threat against
> anyone, especially somebody that's five states over just
> trying to do a job.
>
> So, Judge Lanza, thank you very much again
> for the time. Thank you all for your efforts. I appreciate
> the support. And I appreciate the support that Mr.
> Rissi has in the courtroom today. And I'll go back to
> do my job.[146]

The Court took Mr. Rissi's background and difficulties into account. However, in the end, the judge referred to June 20th phone messages and the seriousness of the threat. The defendant had not only said to Mr. Hickman, "You're going to die," but he left a message with Attorney General Brnovich that "I'm a victim of a crime. That crime was the theft of the 2020 election, the election that was fraudulent across the state of Arizona… fraud data from the Maricopa County Board of Supervisors computer system. Do your job, Brnovich, or you will hang with those sons of b——s at the end. We will see to it. Torches and pitchforks, that's your future, dip s——t."

U.S. District Judge Dominic W. Lanza sentenced Mr. Rissi, 65, to two and a half years in prison and three years of probation after Rissi pleaded guilty to two counts of making interstate threats. Lanza called the threats an "extremely serious offense," and said such threats reverberate through the election system as a whole. Lanza declared,

> Those dissatisfied with election results cannot threaten
> public officials and election officials. This is an
> unambiguous and uncrossable line, and there need to
> be serious consequences.[147]

In January 2024, Jack Sellers was unanimously elected (for another one-year term) as the new Chairman of the Maricopa County Board of Supervisors. He invited the public to support upcoming elections by signing up at GetInvolved.Maricopa.Vote* to become a poll worker, early ballot processor, truck driver, or volunteer. *[elections.maricopa. gov/work-with-us/temporary-positions]

In his "Passing of the Gavel" Address, Sellers said,

> My highest priority in 2024 is to provide our county elections team with the resources and support they need to continue administering lawful, free and fair elections in March, August and November. The eyes of the free world will once again be focused on Maricopa County. I aim to make collaboration and unity among county departments more important than ever before.[148]

The experience in the Senate brought Paul Boyer closer to his personal religious beliefs.

> What matters most is not elected office. But hearing Jesus Himself say to me, "Well done, you good and faithful servant." That is what ultimately matters.

In addition to his letters to the BOS in 2020 and statement to the Court, Clint Hickman re-stated the obvious:

> We don't grade our own homework.

Steve Gallardo quietly reminded us:

> Always go with your heart.

Bill Gates reviewed the job of the Maricopa County BOS—each one having taken the oath or affirmation to uphold the U.S. and Arizona

Constitution—to oversee and canvass, and then certify the results of the 2020 elections:

> The election issues of 2020 were about leadership, not partisan issues. We were a team.

Rusty Bowers, an artist by profession and reserved in demeanor, summed it up clearly:

> I'm against bullying and emotional violence against anybody, especially over the sacredness of our vote. I'd do it again in a heartbeat.

PART SIX

TODAY

"The old world is dying, and the new world struggles to be born.
Now is the time of monsters."

—Antonio Gramsci, from Ben Rhodes,
"How Short-Term Thinking is Destroying America"
The New York Times, % Civic Engagement Beyond Voting (CEBV)

"We must not stumble upon tomorrow, we must build it,
and we all have the responsibility to do so
in a way that responds to the project of God."

—Pope Francis

CHAPTER 30

WHAT IS OUR FUTURE?

Our story is about integrity—not religion, or even politics. I am not Catholic, Jewish, evangelical, atheist, Buddhist, Hindu, or Muslim. Yet, it is clear to me that when we honor those who have acted with integrity, we stand on holy ground.

Whether their "God" is your God, or the Great Spirit, or the Creator, or Jehovah or Allah, or the Om, or the Inner Light, or you are even unsure, the Pope belongs to all of us. The Pope calls us to be our spiritual best. When we act with integrity, we honor what we understand to be "that of God" within us.

What will our future be? Should we listen solely to political pundits? Religious pulpiteers?

I chose these three sources to offer us guidance:

1. Children's stories
2. Thoughts from before Obamacare
3. Our Declaration of Independence

1. Children's stories.

Isaiah said, "And a little child shall lead them." [Isaiah 11:6-9]

The Story of Ferdinand, written by Munro Leaf in 1936, with stunning black-and-white illustrations, describes a peaceful young bull who liked to sit under the cork tree, contemplating the breeze and sniffing at the flowers.

More importantly, Ferdinand followed his conscience. "All the other bulls would run and butt their heads together," but Ferdinand chose his own path. He refused to do what all the other bulls did—even when taken to the big stadium to prove his bull-manship. Ferdinand would not go along with all the others just to fit in. He "sat" his ground. Finally, the matador just stomped with frustration.

It's a message we can appreciate when considering the simple clarity with which some supervisors and legislators refused to "go along with" in the majority of their Republican colleagues.

In 1947, Margaret Wise Brown gave us *Goodnight, Moon.* Have you ever read this book alone? No! You were either a child, reading it with Mom or Dad, or you were Mom or Dad, reading it with your child. How many times have we found—together—the mouse, the fireplace, and the cow jumping over the moon? *Goodnight, Moon* brings people together. A good leader will too.

One of our best classics of all time—and the oldest—is *The Emperor's New Clothes,* written in 1837 by Hans Christian Anderson.

The emperor was obsessed with having more and more new and fancy clothes. Some con men entered his life and started a scam, pretending to weave all sorts of fancy outfits. The emperor would don one of these "outfits" and parade down the street.

The emperor had all the power, so no one wanted to get in his crosshairs. They also didn't want anyone to think them foolish, so everyone went along with the con. They all praised the emperor—and the emperor's new clothes.

Except one child. One day a child attended the parade, looked at the emperor, and said, "The emperor has no clothes!"

Isn't it time to wake up and take notice?

2. "Just for now, not for always."[149]

Before Obamacare provided insurance coverage for pre-existing health conditions, two of my children went uninsured. I began working with a small insurance company, Western Health Services. Our specialty was to obtain partial health insurance coverage for the people who had been denied any coverage by Blue Cross Blue Shield. BCBS had a policy of "three conditions, and you're out." "Mental health issue?" Application declined."

We at WHS found lesser coverage for former police officers with PTSD or divorced women whose ex-husbands had kicked them off the company plan.

We had a motto— "Just for now, not for always." You can get some coverage, just for now. You can't cover your pre-existing conditions, for now, but if there's a broken leg or appendicitis, you're covered. It wasn't great, but it was better than nothing.

By the end of the year, the cop usually had undergone counseling, found another job, and was back on a company-based comprehensive health plan, which also covered his child with special needs. In a similar fashion, the divorcee would learn that work was possible after children grew up, and she would survive a time of partial health insurance coverage— "just for now, not for always"—until she could again obtain a better plan.

We have allowed men and women—who have lied, bullied, encouraged violence, and threatened our democracy—to reach high places of power in government. Currently, most of them are Republican. For example, Kari Lake, with her campaign of lies, lacked the character to become an Arizona governor or senator. From the outset, when Donald Trump made fun of the man with a handicap, then denigrated John McCain, and was overheard bragging, "When you're famous you can do anything with women" including "Grab her by the pussy,"[150] I knew he did not have the character to be President of the United States.

It isn't only about a party. When Ted Kennedy considered a run for the presidency, some Democrats endorsed him. But I recalled the night he was driving home from a party with a young woman— not his wife. The car veered off a little bridge into the river. While Ted managed to escape with his life, Mary Jo Kopechne drowned. Nothing was reported until morning.

President Richard Nixon was caught lying about the planned burglary of the Democratic Headquarters in Watergate, D.C., in

1978. Gary Hart, a Democratic Senator, lost favor after rumors of an extramarital affair.

Democrats have a lot of flaws. But many Republicans have fallen into a rabbit-hole of corruption, lies, bullying, and downright pushing of an anti-Constitutional agenda.

For the many Republicans who care about integrity, it may be time to switch parties—**just for now, not for always.** Neither party is behaving responsibly at this point about big spending or military excess. So, claiming to be "fiscally conservative" is not an excuse to vote for many of the current corrupt Republicans. They *all* voted for the "Big, Beautiful" expensive budget, tax cuts for billionaires, and cuts to Medicaid. Our children and grandchildren will be burdened with our irresponsibility, even if we try to clean up our act starting today.

Republicans who don't want to continue to let autocrats take tyrannical power should take a look at every candidate's integrity. We have witnessed more than mere insults and repeated denigration of others. We have seen repeated lies, threats, and bullying. We have witnessed an active attempt to weaken our electoral systems and deny eligible individuals the right to vote. We have seen mass deportations without due process. We have the military in our streets and attacks on the press.

Please consider a change. It could be to become an Independent, a Libertarian, a "No Labels," or a Democrat. It could be, as suggested by Senator Joe Manchin in his book, *Dead Center,* a new centrist "common sense" American Party. Whatever you do, it should be a solid rejection of the "conservative" right-wing, self-described "Christians," a pro-autocracy group of Republicans who seem to march in lockstep with blatant disregard for our Constitution, laws, and democracy.

Remember, it's just for now, not for always. When we restore ourselves to a Constitutional democracy—and when Republican men and women of good character once again run for high office—you can choose to switch back. Meanwhile, it's time to be something other than a party Republican—**just for now, if not for always.**

3. Our Declaration of Independence.

"We mutually pledge to each other our Lives, our Fortunes, and our sacred Honor."[151]

Most of us are familiar with some of the best lines of the Declaration of Independence:

> When in the course of human events…
>
> We hold these truths to be self-evident, that all men [sic.] are created equal, that they are endowed by their Creator with certain inalienable rights…that to secure these rights, Governments are instituted among Men [sic], deriving their just powers from the consent of the governed.

But most of us do not recall the long list of complaints that the Founding Fathers included in the Declaration against the King of England. To name a few:

- He has refused his Assent to Laws, the most wholesome and necessary for the public good [such as the bipartisan immigration bill before the 2020 election or the peaceful transfer after the valid election results];
- He has refused…to cause others to be elected [you'll be "primary-ed"];
- Made Judges dependent on his Will alone…;
- He has kept among us, in times of peace, Standing Armies without the Consent of our legislatures;
- He has affected to render the Military independent of and superior to the Civil power;
- Quartering large bodies of armed troops among us;

- Protecting [them by pardons] from punishment for and Murders [such as the January 6 riotous assault and trespass] which they should commit on the Inhabitants of these States;
- For cutting off our Trade with all parts of the world [Tariff threats];
- Imposing Taxes [on the majority, with tax breaks to benefit billionaires] without our Consent;
- For depriving us in many cases, of the benefits to Trial by Jury;
- He has excited domestic insurrections amongst us [January 6 assault on the Capitol]; …

A Prince, whose character is thus marked by every act which may define a Tyrant, is unfit to be the ruler of a free people.

We, therefore, …solely publish and declare… And for the support of this Declaration, with a firm reliance on the protection of divine Providence, we mutually pledge to each other our Lives, our Fortunes and our sacred Honor.[152]

The men who formed our nation did not insist on a war. The British caused the war.

We do not need a war. A far better route—for us, today, now—is to restore our time-honored institutions—like the well-run elections conducted by thousands of honorable men and women across this country—and to make peaceful changes needed to secure a safe democracy. Instead of rationalizing bad behavior and going along with the group, it's time for all of us to remember our conscience, our Constitution, our Pledge of Allegiance, and our sacred Honor.

Take a lesson from the playbook of six who stopped the steal.

AFTERWORD

It is hard work to build up a good movement. It is much easier to lie, bully, and tear one down. After the damage, restoring the original structure is a daunting task.

With this book, I attempt to demonstrate the consistent hard work by six men who voted with their conscience to uphold the truth of the 2020 election, and the exemplary efforts made by innumerable others who work the polls for our elections—in Maricopa County and across the country.

Yet some continue to cast aspersions and lies. Others allow themselves to believe the lies.

I invite those of you who, while you may have doubts, want to be open to the truth, to read three books:

People of the Lie: The Hope for Healing Human Evil, by M. Scott Peck, MD, Touchstone, 1983.

The Big Truth: Upholding Democracy in the Age of the Big Lie, by Major Garrett & David Becker, Diversion Books, 2022.

The God of Monkey Science: People of Faith in a Modern Scientific World, by Janet Kellogg Ray, Wm. B. Eerdmans Publishing Co., Grand Rapids, MI, 2023.

People of the Lie explores the concept of evil in what may seem, at first glance, decent and ordinary people. Peck essentially condemns mental or spiritual laziness as morally evil. One example early in the book struck me hard, of a 15-year-old boy placed in a psychiatric hospital after taking the family car and driving it, and himself, into a cement wall at high speed—an attempted suicide.

His parents appeared to be ordinary, decent people. They had jobs and went to church every Sunday. They had chosen to give to their only remaining son, as a Christmas present, after his brother committed suicide the year before, the very same gun with which the brother had killed himself.

What caring parent would do that? What kind of message would it send to the surviving brother? When Peck began asking questions, the couple pulled their son out of counseling.

Peck takes a deep look into what may not seem so bad on the surface, but what, in all its commonness and banality, he believes is evil. Reading his accounts of treating psychiatric patients helps us consider issues more spiritually and seriously. His book, unrelated to politics, speaks profoundly to our self-understanding and our integrity. By reading this book, we may reconsider our own actions in light of new understandings.

The Big Truth, laden with evidence, shows the plan of Donald Trump, many allies, and team members to overthrow the 2020 elections and perpetuate Trump in power. If you like evidence for the basis of making your decisions, you will find this book valuable. While a little thick for the average reader, it's accurate.

The God of Monkey Science is by a woman raised in, and who still believes herself to be deeply connected to, the evangelical Christian tradition. She understands how we can come to accept articles of faith that do not align with scientific evidence. As a science teacher herself, she is comfortable with both. More importantly, she calls out those who would refuse to acknowledge the valid place of science in our world. She understands.

If we read those three books with an open mind, we should come to some new perspectives on the political events described in *Six Who Stopped the Steal.*

ACKNOWLEDGMENTS

People help get a book written. While I can attribute much of *Six Who Stopped the Steal* to documents and research, I was able to write it only with the cooperation and honest participation of many.

Any errors are mine and I'm grateful for the sharp eyes who found some of them.

I felt led to write a story honoring the men who stopped the steal and who were vilified for doing so. Tom Haines and Paulette Gehlker took the time to help me gain clarity that this project was important and I was the one to do it.

My thanks to Scott Bales, who introduced me to Bill Gates and Clint Hickman. Then, a deep thank you to Bill Gates for going into more depth, personally and professionally. My gratitude to Clint Hickman for your inherent decency as well as your sharing of personal information and contacts with others. Thanks to Jack Sellers for many valuable life lessons, and to Rusty Bowers for an honest assessment of his youth and how he learned to become the man he is today. Thanks to Steve Gallardo for your quiet sharing. Paul Boyer, I appreciated the details of those days between the caucus and the vote. I am honored by each of you contributing your candid stories.

Thanks to April Riggins and Ilene Haber in the County Recorder's Office, who gave us a tour of MCTEC—the Maricopa County Ballot Tabulation Center.

Scott Jarrett and Ryan Macias provided me with over-the-top help and guidance on the "weeds" of elections and the voting machinery and process. Sheriff Paul Penzone indicated that the dangers to election officials were probably greater than most of us realized.

Several people deserve special thanks for serving as beta readers. They include Shari Capra, Claude Mattox, and Helen Purcell. Others asked to remain anonymous.

Many others along the way contributed additional understanding, advice, editing guidelines, and evidence to help clarify important concepts, such as cognitive dissonance.

Special thanks to Jen Fifield, journalist; Joe O'Donnell, Brendan Traschel, and Cheryl Hawker.

I returned to Lynn Thompson for editing help after working with her previously, and, true to form, she outdid herself by collaborating with me to clean up this copious and cumbersome collection of information into something coherent and perhaps even understandable.

With great appreciation to Becky Norwood of Spotlight Publishing House and her team for their help in finalizing the publishing process.

Vance, my husband, cheers me on. We know that we must expose the challenges to our democracy caused by fraud and intimidation.

Finally, it is essential to honor those who have served the public with integrity.

QUESTIONS FOR DISCUSSION

1. Consider the events mentioned by each of the six about their youth and what turning points they encountered that led them want to become men of integrity. What stories resonated with you? What did you find unusual? Have you had moments that have influenced who you are or who you want to become?

2. What do we mean by a "monster"? Does the Santa Claus story fit? Do the other examples of "monster" fit—fear of Black people, fear of police, fear of changing religious beliefs? Have you encountered any "monsters" in your life? What kinds of things? How have you dealt with your own "monsters"?

3. Before reading *Six Who Stopped the Steal,* what did you know about your local election process? What did you learn? What are some specific details of elements you had been unaware of? What parts of the process do you believe are most important?

4. What parts of the election process that occurred before the 2020 election season do you believe were most important? Why? What questions do you have about the lead-up to the 2020 elections?

5. What factors make you more likely to believe one speaker over another about election information? Is it their position working in elections? Data? Fear of fraud? One or two personal experiences? Compare notes in a discussion group.

6. Who, other than the Supervisors, the Speaker of the House, and the Senator, seemed to make a significant contribution to making sure officials conducted the elections fairly and accurately, and that the results were certified correctly?

7. There is a lot of evidence that Mr. Trump and various allies and followers planned to prevent the legitimate transfer of power. What do you believe? Why?

8. How many audits, investigations, and hearings were there about the 2020 Maricopa County elections? What was the point of each of them? Who was in charge of each? Why does that matter?

9. What events stuck out during the 2022 elections? What patterns of political behavior persisted?

10. There were hundreds or more threats against various election officials who did what they thought was right. Why do you think this happened? What caused it? Is there a way for things to change?

11. Each of the six did not realize they were making up a final chapter, "Speaking Truth to Power," when they commented about the election situation. Yet each of them gave strong statements about that time. Which one did you like best, and why?

12. What American institutions do you believe are important to preserve American democracy? Why?

VOCABULARY

A.R.S.: Arizona Revised Statutes.

Audit: An official, non-biased, examination and verification of records, usually of financial records, but here, of the accuracy of tabulation of the votes in the election.

Ballot style: A specific ballot layout or content for an election. The ballot style is the presentation of the unique combination of contests and candidates for which the voter is eligible to vote. It includes the order of contests and candidates, the list of ballot positions for each contest, and the binding of candidate names to ballot positions within the presentation. Multiple precincts may use a single ballot style. Multiple styles may appear in a single precinct where voters are split between two or more districts or other categories defining voter eligibility for particular contests and candidates.[153]

BOS: Maricopa County Board of Supervisors.

BTC: Maricopa County Ballot Tabulation Center.

Canvass: Can be both a verb and noun. In the context of elections, the organization responsible for canvassing the elections will give careful scrutiny, or a searching examination, a close and searching look to the tabulated election results, to make sure that all ballots cast are accounted for and that every valid vote cast is included in the final election results. Ultimately there will be an official canvass of the election results. In Maricopa County, and in all other fourteen counties in Arizona, this was the responsibility of the Board of Supervisors, per A.R.S. § 16-642 et seq.

Cognitive dissonance: A mental phenomenon in which we unknowingly hold fundamentally conflicting "cognitions," or ideas, in our mind at the same time. We are confronted by a situation in which our information may—or may not—result in some change to our ideas or actions, reducing the dissonance in our minds.[154]

Confirmation Bias: When you fit all the evidence and observations that are new to you into any pre-existing beliefs you may already possess, whether valid or not.

Conspiracy Theory: A theory that others are planning and plotting in secret something bad that they don't tell us about. A "fake" conspiracy theory is a strategy to confuse the public and bring them to the side of the one alleging something false.

Defamation, Libel, Slander: *Defamation* is the false or unjustified injury of the good reputation of another, intentionally or knowingly, usually with intent. *Libel,* in the law, is defamation by written, printed or broadcast (including social media). *Slander,* in the law, is defamation by oral utterance rather than by writing. In all three—defamation, libel, and slander—the statement is usually malicious, false, and remaining unproved.

Disinformation: False and/or misleading information that is often disseminated by a government or organized group, in a hostile act of tactical political subversion.

Dox or Doxx: To publicly identify or publish private information, often anonymously, often on social media, about someone, for example, a public official, especially as a form of punishment or revenge.

EMS: Election Management System (computers used for elections).

EPM: *Election Procedures Manual* aka *Manual.*

Forensic: Related to, connected with, or used (possibly) in courts of law, especially with reference to the scientific analysis of evidence. In elections it means thorough, expert analysis of the accuracy and reliability of the machines used in the voting process.

Hash Code: A unique code made up of a series and numbers and/or letters assigned to each file and program for the versions of software and applications installed on the certified Election Management System. The applications include tabulation equipment servers, desktop computers, central count tabulators, vote center tabulators, and the adjudication stations.

After a suite of files and programs obtains federal certification, the certified Voting System Testing Laboratory (VSTL) generates a series of unique hash codes using a hash code generator. The hash code generator evaluates each element within each file of the various versions of installed software. After the hash code generator is complete, it assigns the hash codes to that trusted build certified for use by the U.S. Elections Assistance Commission.

Libel: See **Defamation.**

L&A Test: Logic and Accuracy Test. A series of tests that the Elections Department performs on all equipment and all contests. The County (Elections Department) does the tests before each election. The Secretary of State then performs the test. Then, the County (ED) performs another L&A test, which is live-streamed and open to the public. After the election, the Elections department conducts another L&A test to ensure that no changes were made to any software throughout the election—the final step in verifying the election results.

MCSO: Maricopa County Sheriff's Office.

Misinformation: False information that is spread, regardless of whether there is intent to mislead.

OET: Maricopa County Office of Enterprise Technology.

Overvote: A contest in which the voter selected more candidates than allowed for a particular contest (such as voting for two people for President instead of one).

Slander: See **Defamation.**

SOS: Secretary of State.

Source code: Generally understood to mean programming statements that are created by a programmer with a text editor or a visual programming tool and then saved in a file. Object code generally refers to the output, a compiled file, which is produced when the Source Code is compiled with a C compiler.

Splunk Logs: An advanced and scalable software that …analyzes data for operational intelligence.

SWATTING: Making hoax emergency calls to 911 or law enforcement officials to allege a serious ongoing or imminent crime to solicit an armed SWAT response—Special Weapons and Tactics. Such a hoax poses a risk both by creating an emergency at the location and by diverting resources from other public safety duties.

Tabulation: The counting of the votes. Tabulation machines count the vote under the programming of a computer program in the machine.

Tabulation Source Code: One produced specifically for tabulations. See **Source Code.**

FOOTNOTES

Chapter 1

   1   en.wikipedia.org/wiki/Battle_of_the_Bulge

   2   Westlaw: Arizona Court Rules, govt.westlaw.com/azrules/

   3   Arizona Revised Statutes (A.R.S.), § 38-231. Officers and employees required to take loyalty oath, azleg.gov/ars/38/00231.htm

Chapter 4

   4   "Signed by the official." [2] A.R.S. § 38-231. Officers and employees required to take loyalty oath, azleg.gov/ars/38/00231.htm

Chapter 6

   5   Matthew 16:26.

Chapter 7

   6   "Cognitive dissonance," Wikipedia.

   7   *The Big Truth,* p. 51, by Major Garrett and David Becker, Diversion Books, 2022.

   8   Google, "what is a metaphor, grade 5?" and "common metaphors for kids," en.wikipedia.org/wiki/Metaphor

   9   "Yes, Virginia, there is a Santa Claus," en.wikipedia.org/wiki/Yes,_Virginia,_there_is_a_Santa_Claus

Chapter 8

 10 constitution.congress.gov/browse/article-1/section-4/

 11 https://www.azleg.gov/const/arizona_constitution.pdf

 12 A.R.S. § 16-101.

 13 A.R.S. § 16-515(F).

 14 A.R.S. § 16-241©; A.R.S. § 16-645.

 15 A.R.S. § 16-645.

16 A. R. S. § 16-241 ©; A.R.S. § 16-645(B).

Chapter 9

17 en.wikipedia.org/wiki/
COVID-19_pandemic_in_Arizona#January_2020

18 *The God of Monkey Science: People of Faith in a Modern Scientific World,* by Janet Kellogg Ray, Wm. B. Eerdmans Publishing Co., Grand Rapids, MI, 2023.

19 doggett.house.gov/media/blog-post/
timeline-trumps-coronavirus-responses

20 en.wikipedia.org/wiki/George_Floyd_protests

21 *The Big Truth: Upholding Democracy in the Age of THE BIG LIE,* by Major Garrett and David Becker, Diversion Books, 2022, p. 81.

Chapter 10

22 Ibid.

23 nytimes.com/2023/08/17/us/politics/trump-election-lies-fact-check.html

Chapter 13

24 "Statement of Adrian Fontes, Maricopa County Recorder (2016-2020) before the Committee on House Administration," U.S. House of Representatives, July 28, 2020.

Chapter 16

25 "Help America Vote Act," United States Election Assistance Commission, eac.gov/about/help_america_vote_act.aspx

26 Google, "Maricopa County Supervisors take responsibility from County Recorder." maricopa.gov/5410/Biography; recorder.maricopa.gov/about-us/about-the-office-and-recorder.html in conversation with Bill Gates, l6/27/25.

27 azcleanelections.gov/arizona-elections for "Madison Elementary 38 School District."

28 maricopa.gov/CivicAlerts.aspx?AID-924&ARC for "Maricopa County Officials Approve Presidential Preference Election Plans."

Chapter 18

29 The Big Truth, by Major Garrett and David Becker, Diversion Books, 2022, pp. 16-17.

30 Ibid.

31 swalwell.house.gov/issues/russia-trump-his-administration-s-ties

32 en.wikipedia.org/wiki/Attempts_to_overturn_the_2020_United_States_presidential_election

33 Ibid.

34 en.wikipedia.org/wiki/Adrian_Fontes and en.wikipedia.org/wiki/Stephen_Richer

35 Supra, Attempts to Overturn.

36 Ibid.

37 Ibid.

Chapter 19

38 stacks.cdc.gov/view/cdc/85526

39 "Timeline of Trump's Coronavirus Responses," Blog Post, March 22, 2022.

40 "Governor Doug Ducey Issues Declaration of Emergency, Executive Order to Combat Continued spread of COVID-19" (March 11, 2020). content.govdelivery.com/accounts/AZMARIC/bulletins/280da07

41 "COVID-19 and Election Impacts—Message from Supervisor Gates, March 13, 2020," maricopa.gov/CivicAlerts.aspx?AID=1025&ARC=3004

42 "I'm sorry, I can't do this," FOX 10 Phoenix, Arizona, youtube.com/watch?v=hsT15qLqkAg with Scott Jarrett, the Maricopa County, Arizona Election Day Director, walks away from the podium during a news report regarding the March 17, 2020, Presidential Preference Election.

43 en.wikipedia.org/wiki/
    COVID-19_pandemic_in_Arizona#January_2020

44 azcentral.com/story/news/local/phoenix/2020/06/19/
    maricopa-county-requires-masks-countywide-curb-spread-
    covid-19/3227812001/ for "Maricopa County sends mandate
    to every resident in the county…" by Pauline Pineda, Joshua
    Bowling, Alison Steinbach, Lorraine Longhe and Sasha Hupka,
    Arizona Republic, June 19, 2020.

45 Ibid.

Chapter 20

46 maricopa.gov/5539/Voting-Equipment-Fact

47 Ibid.

48 A.R.S. § 16-661.A.

49 Ibid.

50 Supra, Voting-Equipment-Facts

Chapter 21

51 "Comments" email from Helen Purrcell, former County recorder,
    October 22, 2025.

52 cnbc.com/2020/11/07/trump-refuses-to-accept-election-results-
    says-it-is-far-from-over.html by Kevin Breuninger.

53 "Statement of Adrian Fontes, Maricopa County Recorder (2016-
    2020) before the Committee on House Administration," U.S.
    House of Representatives, July 28, 2020.

54 Ibid.

55 "After harassment, Arizona county official won't run for
    reelection," June 1, 2023, by Yvonne Wingettt Sanchez,
    Democracy in America; "A Thank You to Bill Gates," by Robert
    Robb, azcentral.com, June 2, 2025.

56 "Arizona official targeted by election deniers now struggles with
    PTSD," by Yvonne Wingett Sanchez, Democracy in America,
    Washington Post, May 6, 2023.

57 en.wikipedia.org/wiki/Adrian_Fontes (6/21/25).

58 "Statement of Adrian Fontes, Maricopa County Recorder (2016-2020) before the Committee on House Administration," U.S. House of Representatives, July 28, 2020.

Chapter 22

59 content.govdelivery.com/accounts/AZMARIC/bulletins/28336ea with "All ballots have been counted in Maricopa County for the March 17 Presidential Preference Election, March 26, 2020.

60 Emails from Gates, Hickman, and Sellers to NHM, August 26, 2025.

61 maricopa.gov/DocumentCenter/View/64676/PR69-11-17-20-Letter-to-Voters from Chairman Clint Hickman, November 17, 2020.

62 Conversation between Bill Gates and NHM, June 20, 2025; email from Hickman to NHM August 26, 2025.

63 Conversation between Bill Gates and NHM, June 20, 2025.

64 Rusty Bowers conversations with NHM, June 20 and 21, 2025.

65 "Russell 'Rusty' Bowers," 2022 Profile in Courage Award, John F. Kennedy Presidential Library and Museum.

66 Boyer conversations with and emails to NHM on August 23 and 25, 2025; "Arizona Senate Republicans are abusing their subpoena power. Strip them of it," by Robert Robb, *Arizona Republic,* February 8, 2021.

Chapter 23

67 "Statement of Adrian Fontes, Maricopa County Recorder (2016-2020) before the Committee on House Administration," U.S. House of Representatives, July 28, 2020.

68 Ibid.

69 Hickman email to NHM, August 26, 2025.

70 Wingett Sanchez, May 6, 2023, *Washington Post.* See also footnote 71.

71 oversightdemocrats.house.gov/sites/evo-subsites/democrats on October 7, 2021, Testimony of Bill Gates before the U.S. House Oversight Committee.

Chapter 24

72 azcentral.com/story/news/politics/electionos/2021/0226/judge-says-maricops-county-must-provide-2020-ballots-arizona-senate/6835892002 for "Judge Rules Maricopa County must provide 2020 ballots to Arizona Senate for audit under subpoenas," Jen Fifield, Arizona Republic, Feb. 26, 2021.

73 A.R.S. § 16-624.B.

74 maricopa.gov/5681/Elections-Equipment-Audit in 2021.

75 "Update on Forensic Audit of Maricopa County's Tabulation Equipment," from Scott Jarrett, Director of Election Day and Emergency Voting, and Rey Valenzuela, Director of Election Services and Early Voting, to the Maricopa County Board of Supervisors, February 23, 2021.

76 Ibid.

77 "Maricopa County Procurement Evaluation Voting System and Related Equipment," by Berry Dunn, to the Maricopa County Board of Supervisors, July 2021.

78 maricopa.gov/CivicAlerts.aspx?AID=2690 for "Printer Investigation Complete," April 10, 2023.

Chapter 25

79 "Judge Rules Maricopa County must provide 2020 ballots to Arizona Senate for audit under subpoenas," Jen Fifield, Arizona Republic, Feb. 26, 2021.

80 azmirror.com/2020/11/12/stephen-richer-wins-maricopa-county-recorder-race-fontes-concedes/

81 "Arizona official targeted by election deniers now struggles with PTSD," by Yvonne Wingett Sanchez, May 6, 2023, *Washington Post;* emails from Paul Boyer, September and October 2025.

82 A.R.S. § 624. A., B., D., Disposition of official returns and ballots.

83 "Judge Rules Maricopa County must provide 2020 ballots to Arizona Senate for audit under subpoenas," Jen Fifield, *Arizona Republic,* February 26, 2021; Hon. Timothy J. Thomason, CV 2020-016840, Conclusion, February 25, 2021.

84 Ibid., Thomason.

85 Supra, Fifield.

86 Ibid.

87 cnn.com/2021/06/17/politics/arizona-audit-cyber-ninjas-logan-invs for "Arizona 2020 ballot review to be made public September 24," by Adam Brewster, *CBS News,* September 17, 2021.

88 Ibid.

89 Ibid.

90 "Arizona official targeted by election deniers now struggles with PTSD," by Yvonne Wingett Sanchez, *Washington Post,* May 6, 2023.

91 Supra, Brewster.

92 Arizona_prosecution_of_fake_electors

93 content.govdelivery.com/accounts/AZMARIC/bulletins/30ff7ce for "Chairman Gates Responds to Latest Subpoena Related to Elections," by Maricopa County Supervisor Bill Gates 3/22/2022.

94 Email from Maricopa County Board of Supervisors to Committee on Oversight and Reform, U.S. House of Representatives, November 1, 2021.

95 maricopa.gov/DocumentCenter/View/74501/Final-Report-Answers-to-Senate-Questions on March 23, 2022. [appears to be archived or deleted]

96 Ibid.

Chapter 26

97 House Jan. 6 Committee Hearings: "Arizona Lawmaker Rusty Bowers details the pressure put on him by Trump and Giuliani," by Ximena Bustillo, June 21, 2022, NPR.

98 Bowers conversation with NHM, July 23, 2025.

99 "Arizona official targeted by election deniers now struggles with PTSD," by Yvonne Wingett Sanchez, *Washington Post,* May 6, 2023.

100 azcentral.com/story/opinion/oped/laurieroberts/2024/02/15/clint-hickman-reelection-few-republicans-balk-trump/72617849007/

101 Statement by Donald J. Trump, 45th President of the United States of America, July 22, 2021.

102 Supra, Laurie Roberts.

103 All individuals quoted and/or mentioned are cited in *The Big Truth,* by Major Garrett and David Becker, Diversion Books, 2022, pp. 94-96 and 134-176.

104 Ibid., *The Big Truth,* p. 115.

Chapter 27

105 stanton.house.gov/2025/6/stanton-takes-kari-lake-to-task-over-repeated-election-lies-at-house-foreign-affairs-committee-hearing

106 Ibid.

107 "Arizona official targeted by election deniers now struggles with PTSD," by Yvonne Wingett Sanchez, *Washington Post,* May 6, 2023.

108 JenFifield@votebeat.org, email July 18, 2025.

109 Supra, Yvonne Wingett-Sanchez.

110 politico.com/news/2023/06/01/key-arizona-election-official-step-down-00099752 by Madison Fernandez.

111 Ibid.

112 Supra, Stanton.

113 Gates' conversation with NHM, President Trump's Tweet, June 20, 2025.

114 cbsnews.com/news/conservative-channel-newsmax-settlement-dominion-voting-systems-defamation-case/

115 Ibid.

116 Donald J. Trump @realDonaldTrump. ℅ Maricopa County Democratic Party, August 18, 2025.

117 "Free Enterprise Club argues that fewer comparison signatures from voters mean better elections," by Caitlin Sievers, *AZMirror*, August 20, 2025.

118 votebeat.org/arizona/2025/09/22/maricopa-county-recorder-justin-heap-releases-text-messages-supervisors/

Chapter 28

119 en.wikipedia.org/wiki/Dominion_Voting_Systems_v._Fox_News_Network

120 Email letter to Arizona Senate President Karen Fann, May 17, 2021, from Maricopa County Supervisors Jack Sellers, Chairman; Bill Gates, Vice Chairman, Steve Chucri, Clint Hickman, and Steve Gallardo; Stephen Richer, Maricopa County Recorder; and Paul Penzone, Maricopa County Sheriff.

121 justice.gov/d9/2023-08/Memorandum-Guidance-Re-Threats-Elections-Workers.pdf on June 25, 2021, Deputy Attorney General, Washington, D.C.

122 "Correcting the Record, Maricopa County's In-Depth Analysis of the Senate Inquiry," by the Maricopa County Elections Department and the Office of the Recorder, January 2022.

123 stanton.house.gov/2025/6/stanton-takes-kari-lake-to-task-over-repeated-election-lies-at-house-foreign-affairs-committee-hearing

124 Ibid.

125 "Man sentenced after threats to county leader," by Sasha Hupka, *Arizona Republic,* January 31, 2024.

126 "Maricopa County supervisors unanimously reappoint elections director and give him a new boss," by Sasha Hupka, azcentral.com, June 29, 2023.

127 Ibid.

128 azmirror.com/2024/11/17/kari-lake-settles-defamation-suit-with-maricopa-county-recorder-stephen-richer/

129 Ibid.

130 theguardian.com/us-news/2024/mar/27/
kari-lake-defamation-lawsuit

131 azmirror.com/2024/11/17/kari-lake-settles-defamation-suit-
with-maricopa-county-recorder-stephen-richer/

132 JenFifield@votebeat.org email, July 18, 2025.

133 en.wikipedia.org/wiki/Arizona_prosecution_of_fake_electors

134 Ibid.

135 politico.com/news/2025/08/05/
trump-fake-electors-cases-00494884

136 stanton.house.gov/2025/6/stanton-takes-kari-lake-to-task-over-
repeated-election-lies-at-house-foreign-affairs-committee-hearing

137 cbsnews.com/news/conservative-channel-newsmax-settlement-
dominion-voting-systems-defamation-case/

138 Ibid.

Chapter 29

139 maricopa.gov/DocumentCenter/View/64399/PR68-11-4-20-
Letter-to-Voters from Clint Hickman and Steve Gallardo.

140 youtube.com/live/XUHPaJWiG68?si= Maricopa County Special
Meeting, November 20, 2020.

141 Statement from Paul Boyer to the Arizona Senate, February 8,
2021.

142 House Jan. 6 Committee Hearings: "Arizona Lawmaker Rusty
Bowers details the pressure put on him by Trump and Giuliani,"
by Ximena Bustillo, June 21, 2022, NPR.

143 Mr. Jack Sellers Testimony: "Hearing on the Arizona Election
'Audit,'" U.S. House Oversight Committee, October 7, 2021
(YouTube and print-out of Sellers' remarks).

144 oversightdemocrats.house.gov/sites/evo-subsites/democrats-
oversight.house.gov/files/Gates%20Testimony.pdf on October 7,
2021, Testimony of Bill Gates before the U.S. House Oversight
Committee; Sellers, Gates:

oversightdemocrats.house.gov/news/press-releases/
oversight-committee-hearing-exposes-how-arizona-election-
audit-aimed-to

145 maricopa.gov/CivicAlerts.aspx?AID=2690 for "Printer
Investigation Complete, April 10, 2023.

146 Reporter's Transcript of Proceedings Sentencing Hearing, United
States of America, Plaintiff, vs. Mark Anthony Rissi, Defendant,
Statement by Clint Hickman, U.S. District Court for the
District of Arizona, August 28, 2023.

147 votebeat.org/arizona/2023/8/29/23850868/mark-rissi-prison-
sentence-arizona-election-worker-threats/ for "'I just hope
it ends': Maricopa official shares emotional story as harasser
sentenced to prison," Jen Fifield, *Votebeat,* August 29, 2023.

148 maricopa.gov/CivicAlerts.aspx?AIS=2856 for "Jack Sellers
Elected Chairman of Maricopa County Board of Supervisors,"
January 3, 2024.

Chapter 30

149 Cheryl Hawker, Western Health Services, 1990.

150 bbc.com/news/election-us-2016-37595321

151 Thomas Jefferson and colleagues, July 4, 1776.

152 *Declaration of Independence,* July 4, 1776, the Rotunda at the
National Archives Museum.

Vocabulary

153 lawinsider.com/dictionary/ballot-style

154 "Cognitive dissonance," Wikipedia

RESOURCES AND BIBLIOGRAPHY

Some links that are no longer be available and
may have been archived or deleted.

Books and Pamphlets

On Tyranny: Twenty Lessons from the Twentieth Century, by Timothy Snyder, Tim Duggan Books, New York, NY, 2017.

People Of the Lie, by M. Scott Peck, M.D., Touchstone, NY, 1983, p. 47-61.

Plain Living: A Quaker Path to Simplicity, by Catherine Whitmire, Sorin Books, 2001, p. 30.

The Big Truth: Upholding Democracy in the Age of THE BIG LIE, by Major Garrett and David Becker, Diversion Books, 2022.

The God of Monkey Science: People of Faith in a Modern Scientific World, by Janet Kellogg Ray, Wm. B. Eerdmans Publishing Co., Grand Rapids, MI, 2023.

The Light We Carry: Overcoming in Uncertain Times, by Michelle Obama, Crown Trade Paperback Edition, 2024.

Conversations, Emails, Letters, and Interviews

(NHM = Nancy Hicks Marshall)

- "Comments" email to NHM from Helen Purcell, former County Recorder, October 23, 2025.
- Conversation with and emails from Rusty Bowers to NHM, July and August 2025.

- Conversation with and emails from Boyer to NHM, August, September, and October 2025.
- Conversation with and emails from Bill Gates to NHM, June 20, and July, August, September, and October 2025.
- Conversation with Steve Gallardo, August 20, 2025.
- Conversations with and emails from Clint Hickman to NHM, June, July, August, September, and October 2025.
- Conversation with and emails from Jack Sellers to NHM, July and August 2025.

Email to Committee on Oversight and Reform, U.S. House of Representatives, from Maricopa County Board of Supervisors, November 1, 2021.

Email letter to Arizona Senator Boyer, January 19, 2021, from Vice-Chairman of the BOS, Bill Gates.

Email letter to Arizona Senate President Karen Fann, May 17, 2021, from Maricopa County Supervisors Jack Sellers, Chairman; Bill Gates, Vice Chairman, Steve Chucri, Clint Hickman, Steve Gallardo; and Stephen Richer, Maricopa County Recorder; and Paul Penzone, Maricopa County Sheriff.

Jenfifield@votebeat.org email, July 18, 2025.

Letter from Clint Hickman, Chairman, and Steve Gallardo, Supervisor, District 5, Maricopa County Board of Supervisors, to Maricopa County voters, November 4, 2020.

Letter from Clint Hickman, BOS Chairman, to Maricopa County Voters, November 17, 2020.

Paul Boyer Statement to Arizona Senate, February 8, 2021.

Visit by NHM and others to MCTEC Maricopa County Technical and Elections Center, two-hour tour of all equipment and processes, provided by Ilene Haber and April Riggins, permanent staff at the Recorder's Office, August 20, 2025.

Constitutions, Laws, Court Rules, and Court Cases

Arizona Constitution, Article II. Declaration of Rights.

Arizona Constitution and Revised Statutes Annotated, August, 2014: A.R.S. § 16-661.

A.R.S. § 16-101, No Residence Address Confirmation.

A.R.S. § 16-121.B., No Residence Address Confirmation.

A.R.S. § 16-168.F., Precinct Registers; Violation.

A.R.S. § 16-241; A.R.S. § 16-645; A.R.S. § 16-648. County Board of Supervisors Canvassing Duties; Secretary of State Canvassing Duties.

A.R.S. § 16-515. Observer Guidelines.

A.R.S. § 16-541. Early Voting.

A.R.S. § 16-542. Request for ballot, azleg.gov/ars/16/00542.htm

A.R.S. § 16-624. A., B., D., Disposition of official returns and ballots.

A.R.S. § 16-661 (post-2020).

A.R.S. § 38-231. Officers and employees required to take loyalty oath, azleg.gov/ars/38/00231.htm

A.R.S. § 41-1153. Disobedience of subpoena as legislative contempt.

A.R.S. § 41-1155. Offenses punishable by legislature; limitation on imprisonment, azleg.gov/ars/41/01155.htm

CV 2020-016840, *MARICOPA COUNTY, et al., v. KAREN FANN, et al,* 2/25/2021: Minute Entry, Later: Background, Scope of the Ruling, Validity of the Subpoenas, Conclusion.

"Declaration of Independence: A Transcription," National Archives. July 4, 1776. azleg.gov/const/arizona_constitution.pdf

govt.westlaw.com/azrules/Index for ER 8. 1. Bar Admission and Disciplinary Matters; Preamble, A Lawyer's Responsibilities, Effective January 1, 2025.

reaganlibrary.gov/constitutional-amendments-amendment-12-electing-president-and-vice-president

United States Constitution Annotated, Article 1, Section 4, Clause 1—Elections Clause.

United States of America, Plaintiff, vs. Mark Anthony Rissi, Defendant, No. 2:22-cr-01283-DWL, Phoenix, Arizona, before: The Honorable Dominic W. Lanza, Judge, Reporter's Transcript of Proceedings, Sentencing Hearing, August 28, 2023.

Online Links and References

Based on the quantity of research, there may be duplication or updates.

abc15.com/news/local-news/arizona-lawmaker-proposes-giving-legislature-not-voters-final-say-on-presidential-winner posted in January 2024.

"After harassment, Arizona county official won't run for reelection," by Yvonne Wingettt Sanchez, *Democracy in America. Washington Post,* June 1, 2023.

"All ballots have been counted in Maricopa County for the March 17 Presidential Preference Election," *Granicus,* content.govdelivery.com, Phoenix, March 26, 2020.

"Answers to Senate Questions Regarding Maricopa County Election Network: Arizona 2020 Presidential Election," by Former Congressman John Shadegg, Special Master, March 23, 2022.

"Arizona lawmaker Rusty Bowers details the pressure put on him by Trump and Giuliani," by Ximena Bustillo, *NPR,* House Jan. 6 Committee Hearings, June 21, 2022.

"Arizona official targeted by election deniers now struggles with PTSD," by Yvonne Wingett Sanchez, *Washington Post,* May 6, 2023.

Arizona Secretary of State 2023 *Election Procedures Manual.*

"Arizona senate Republicans are abusing their subpoena power. Strip them of it," by Robert Robb, *Arizona Republic,* February 5, 2021.

"Arizona 2020 ballot review to be made public September 24," by Adam Brewster, *CBS News,* September 17, 2021.

"A thank you to Bill Gates," by Robert Robb, azcentral.com, posted on June 2, 2023.

azcentral.com/story/news/politics/electionos/2021/0226/judge-says-maricops-county-must-provide-2020-ballots-arizona-senate/6835892002 for "Judge Rules Maricopa County must provide 2020 ballots to Arizona Senate for audit under subpoenas," written by Jen Fifield, *Arizona Republic,* February 26, 2021.

azcentral.com/story/opinion/op-ed/ej-montini/2022/01/10/karen-fann-failings-arizona-election-audit-worse-cyber-ninjas/9154349002/

azcentral.com/story/opinion/op-ed/laurieroberts/2024/02/15/clint-hickman-reelection-few-republicans-balk-trump/72617849007/

azcentral.com/story/news/local/phoenix/2020/06/19/maricopa-county-requires-masks-countywide-curb-spread-covid-19/3227812001/ for "Maricopa County sends mandate to every resident in the county…" by Pauline Pineda, Joshua Bowling, Alison Steinbach, Lorraine Longhe, and Sasha Hupka, *Arizona Republic,* June 19, 2020.

azcleanelections.gov/arizona-elections for "Madison Elementary 38 School District."

azmirror.com/2020/11/12/stephen-richer-wins-maricopa-county-recorder-race-fontes-concedes/

azmirror.com/2020/12/15/senate-issues-subpoenas-for-all-ballots-voting-machines-to-audit-maricopa-county-election/

azmirror.com/2021/09/17/
county-senate-reach-agreement-to-end-subpoena-fight-over-routers/

azmirror.com/2023/08/29/i-just-hope-it-ends-maricopa-official-
shares-emotional-story-as-harasser-sentenced-to-prison/

azmirror.com/2024/11/17/kari-lake-settles-defamation-suit-with-
maricopa-county-recorder-stephen-richer/

azmirror.com/2025/08/20/free-enterprise-club-argues-that-fewer-
comparison-signatures-from-voters-mean-better-elections/

azpbs.org/horizon/2021/11/former-member-maricopa-county-board-
about-his-resignation/ (regarding Steve Chucri).

azsenaterepublicans.gov/post/arizona-senate-hires-auditor-to-review-
2020-election-in-maricopa-county

azsos.gov/elections/about-elections/elections-procedures/epm

ballotpedia.org/Stephen_Richer (printed June 20, 2025).

"Bill Gates, Key Arizona election official, won't run for re-election
amid harassment," by Madison Fernandez, *POLITICO,* June 1, 2023.

"Board Approves Mask Regulations Due to Community Spread of
COVID-19, Maricopa County Office of Communications," posted
on June 19, 2020.

"Board Leaders Respond to 'Absurd' Lawsuit from County Recorder,"
maricopa.gov/CivicAlerts.aspx?AID=3346 from the Office of
Communications and posted on June 12, 2025.

"Board of Supervisors Stands up for Election Integrity, Stops Recorder's Misguided Ballot Plan," from the Office of Communications, maricopa.gov/CivicAlerts.aspx?AID-3305 and posted May 5, 2025.

cbsnews.com/news/conservative-channel-newsmax-settlement-dominion-voting-systems-defamation-case/

cbsnews.com/news/maricopa-election-officials-work-to-restore-belief-in-ballot-60-minutes-transcript/

cdc.gov/museum/timeline/covid19.html

"Chairman Jack Sellers Recognized for Empowering Women in Transportation," from maricopa.gov, printed June 25, 2025.

chandlernews.com/santan/news/drama-in-gop-supervisor-race/article_2025642c-f387-11ee-bede-93a156f08328.html (regarding Jack Sellers).

"Chris, Krebs, ex-head of cybersecurity agency targeted by Trump, has Global Entry membership revoked," by Melissa Quinn, *CBS News,* updated May 1, 2025.

"Clint Hickman Elected Chairman of Maricopa County Board of Supervisors," posted in 2023 from maricopa.gov/CivicAlerts.aspx?AID=2644 printed on June 25, 2025.

cnn.com/2021/06/17/politics/arizona-audit-cyber-ninjas-logan-invs for "Arizona 2020 ballot review to be made public September 24," by Adam Brewster, September 17, 2021, *CBS News.*

"Cognitive Dissonance," en.wikipedia.org/wiki/Cognitive_dissonance printed June 27, 2025.

"Common metaphors for kids," en.wikipedia.org/wiki/Metaphor

congress.gov/117/meeting/house/114111/documents/HHRG-117-GO00-20211007-SD001.pdf

content.govdelivery.com/accounts/AZMARIC/bulletins/28336ea for "All ballots have been counted in Maricopa County for the March 17 Presidential Preference Election," March 26, 2020.

content.govdelivery.com/accounts/AZMARIC/bulletins/30ff7ce for "Chairman Gates Responds to Latest Subpoena Related to Elections," by Maricopa County Supervisor Bill Gates, March 22, 2022.

content.govdelivery.com/accounts/AZMARIC/bulletins/28336ea in Phoenix, "All ballots have been counted in Maricopa County for the March 17 Presidential Preference Election," March 26, 2020.

"Correcting the Record, Maricopa County's In-Depth Analysis of the Senate Inquiry," by the Maricopa County Elections Department and the Office of the Recorder, January, 2022.

"Critic of Arizona's elections operations unseats incumbent election official in GOP primary," by Jacques Billeaud, Gabriel Sandoval and Sejal Govindarao, *Associated Press, Arizona Daily Sun,* Thursday, August 1, 2024.

doggett.house.gov/media/blog-post/timeline-trumps-coronavirus-responses

"Dominion Voting Systems v. Fox News Network," en.wikipedia.org/wiki/Dominion_Voting_Systems_v._Fox_News posted in 2023.

"Election Subversion: A Growing Threat to Election Integrity," Statement of Adrian Fontes, Maricopa County Recorder (2016-2020)

Before the Committee on House Administration, U.S. House of Representatives, dated July 28, 2020. [Possibly 2021.]

en.wikipedia.org/wiki/Adrian_Fontes [accessed June 21, 2025]

en.wikipedia.org/wiki/Arizona_prosecution_of_fake_electors

en.wikipedia.org/wiki/Attempts_to_overturn_the_2020_United_States_presidential_election

en.wikipedia.org/wiki/Battle_of_the_Bulge

en.wikipedia.org/wiki/Cognitive_dissonance

en.wikipedia.org/wiki/COVID-19_pandemic_in_Arizona#January_2020

en.wikipedia.org/wiki/Criticism_of_the_government_response_to_Hurricane_Katrina

en.wikipedia.org/wiki/Dominion_Voting_Systems_v._Fox_News_Network

en.wikipedia.org/wiki/George_Floyd_protests

en.wikipedia.org/wiki/Maggie_Haberman

en/wikipedia.org/wiki/metaphor

en.wikipedia.org/wiki/Russell_Bowers

en.wikipedia.org/wiki/Stephen_Richer

en.wikipedia.org/wiki/Steve_Gallardo [accessed June 26, 2025] en.wikipedia.org/wiki/Trump_fake_electors_plot

en.wikipedia.org/wiki/United_States_Electoral_College

en.wikipedia.org/wiki/Yes,_Virginia,_there_is_a_Santa_Claus

"Fact-Checking the Breadth of Trump's Election Lies," by Linda Qiu, *New York Times,* August 17, 2023.

"Forcing Arizona businesses to take cash is not very GOP," in "Your Turn," by Stephen Richer, *Arizona Republic,* March 16, 2025.

"Free Enterprise Club argues that fewer comparison signatures from voters mean better elections," by Caitlin Sievers, *AZMirror,* posted on August 20, 2025.

"Governor Doug Ducey Issues Declaration of Emergency, Executive Order to Combat Continued spread of COVID-19," by Governor Ducey, March 11, 2020. content.govdelivery.com/accounts/AZMARIC/bulletins/280da07

"Help America Vote Act," United States Election Assistance Commission, June 7, 2023.

"Horrible GOP absolutely deserves a place at ASU," in "Your Turn," by Stephen Richer, *Arizona Republic,* Saturday, February 8, 2025.

House Jan. 6 Committee Hearings: "Arizona Lawmaker Rusty Bowers details the pressure put on him by Trump and Giuliani," by Ximena Bustillo, *NPR,* June 21, 2022.

"'I Just hope it ends': Maricopa official shares emotional story as harasser sentenced to prison, Clint Hickman described the effect of threats on him and his family, while the perpetrator said he was misled by election lies," by Jen Fifield, *Votebeat,* August 29, 2023. azmirror.com/2023/08/29/i-just-hope-it-ends-maricopa-official-shares-emotional-story-as-harasser-sentenced-to-prison/

Information Packet from the Maricopa County Elections Department and the Maricopa County Recorder's Office, distributed by MCTEC, August 20, 2025.

"Is climate change worsening fires, storms?" by Joan Meiners, Climate Reporter, *Arizona Republic, USA Today Network,* published on August 3, 2025.

"Jack Sellers Elected Chairman of Maricopa County Board of Supervisors," mcdot.maricopa.gov/m/NewsFlash/Home/Detail/2856 posted on January 3, 2024.

jfklibrary.org/events-and-awards/profile-in-courage-award/award-recipients/defending-democracy-2022/russell-rusty-bowers

"Judge rules Maricopa County must provide 2020 ballots to Arizona Senate for audit under subpoenas," by Jen Fifield, *Arizona Republic,* February 26, 2021.

justice.gov/d9/2023-08/Memorandum-Guidance-Re-Threats-Elections-Workers.pdf from Deputy Attorney General, Washington, D.C. on June 25, 2021.

"Kari Lake signaled on Tuesday," theguardian.com/us-news/2024/mar/27/kari-lake-defamation-lawsuit by Sam Levine, posted on March 27, 2024.

ktar.com/arizona-news/republican-maricopa-county-supervisor-steve-chucri-stepping-down-cites-political-toxicity/4692450/

lawinsider.com/dictionary/ballot-style

"Man sentenced after threats to county leader," by Sasha Hupka, *Arizona Republic*, January 31, 2024.

"Maricopa County Election Facts: Voting Equipment & Accuracy" from maricopa.gov/5539/Voting-Equipment-Facts and accessed on June 24, 2025.

"Maricopa County Officials Approve Presidential Preference Election Plans," maricopa.gov/CivicAlerts.aspx?AID=924&ARC=1755 on December 12, 2019. [archived]

"Maricopa County Procurement Evaluation Voting System and Related Equipment," by Berry Dunn, to the Maricopa County Board of Supervisors, July 2021.

"Maricopa County Recorder turns over texts sought by vote beat about his fight for election authority," by Jen Fifield, *Votebeat*, on July 30, 2025.

"Maricopa County Supervisor Clint Hickman won't seek re-election," kjzz.org/2024-02-15/content-1871418-maricopa-county-supervisor-clint-hickman-wont-seek-reelection by Wayne Schutsky, posted on May 17, 2024.

"Maricopa County supervisors unanimously reappoint elections director and give him a new boss," by Sasha Hupka, azcentral.com, June 29, 2023.

maricopa.gov/DocumentCenter/View/66842/
Forensic-Audit-Transmittal-Letter

azmirror.com/2022/03/23/shadegg-report-from-audit-finds-no-internet-connection-for-ballot-tabulation-equipment/ posted on March 23, 2022.

maricopa.gov/5410/Biography for Supervisor Brophy McGee.

maricopa.gov/5681/Elections-Equipment-Audit in 2021.

"Mr. Jack Sellers Testimony: Hearing on the Arizona Election 'Audit'," U.S. House Oversight Committee, YouTube and Printout of Sellers' remarks, October 7, 2021.

"NASPA POLICY AND PRACTICE SERIES: Safe Spaces and Brave Spaces," by Diana Ali, NASPA Research and Policy Institute, Issue 2, October 2017.

"Newsmax to pay $67 million settlement in Dominion Voting Systems defamation case," *CBS News,* August 18, 2025.

"No wonder voters hate elections. Campaigns never end," in "Your Turn," by Stephen Richer, *Arizona Republic,* February 1, 2025.

nytimes.com/2023/08/17/us/politics/trump-election-lies-fact-check.html

"Opinion: Maricopa County Supervisor Clint Hickman says he won't run for re-election. Who can blame him, after all the threats heaped upon him by the trump mob?" by Laurie Roberts, *Arizona Republic,* February 15, 2024.

oversightdemocrats.house.gov/news/press-releases/oversight-committee-hearing-exposes-how-arizona-election-audit-aimed-to oversightdemocrats.house.gov/sites/evo-subsites/democrats-oversight.house.gov/files/Gates%20Testimony.pdf with the Testimony of Bill Gates before the U.S. Congressional House Oversight Committee, October 7, 2021.

"Part 2: Voter Registration & Mail Voting," from the Maricopa County Recorder's Office, maricopa.gov printed June 25, 2025.

"Paul Boyer statement to the Arizona Senate," February 8, 2021.

"Pew Research Center analysis of COVID-19 data collected," pewresearch.org/politics/2022/03/03/the-changing-political-geography-of-covid-19-over-the-last-two-years/ by the *New York Times*, as of February 28, 2022.

politico.com/news/2023/06/01/key-arizona-election-official-step-down-00099752

politico.com/news/2025/08/05/trump-fake-electors-cases-00494884

"Printer Investigation Complete," Ruth McGregor Report, maricopa.gov/CivicAlerts.aspx?AID=2690 on April 10, 2023.

recorder.maricopa.gov/about-us/about-the-office-and-recorder.html on November 25, 2024.

"Republican County Supervisor Jack Sellers lost his primary. Now he's endorsing a Democrat," by Wayne Schutsky, *KJZZ*, produced on September 18, 2024.

search.asu.edu/profile/4888744 for William (Bill) Gates, printed on June 26, 2025.

"Stanton Takes Kari Lake to Task Over Repeated Election Lies at House Foreign Affairs Committee Hearing," stanton.house. gov/2025/6/stanton-takes-kari-lake-to-task-over-repeated-election-lies-at-house-foreign-affairs-committee-hearing on June 25, 2025.

"State election officials prepared to sue: Some counties could refuse to certify results," by Erin Mansfield, *USA Today*, azcentral.com, September 25, 2024.

Statement by Donald J. Trump, 45th President of the United States of America, regarding Arizona State Senator Paul Boyer, July 22, 2021.

"Statement of Adrian Fontes, Maricopa County Recorder (2016-2020) before the Committee on House Administration," U.S. House of Representatives, July 28, 2020.

statesunited.org/wp-content/uploads/2021/01/000A-Myths-and-Facts-of-the-2020-Presidential-Election-20210113-FINAL-2.pdf

"Stephen Richer shows us how to lose the right way," by Laurie Roberts, *Arizona Republic, USA Today Network*, August 3, 2024.

swalwell.house.gov/issues/russia-trump-his-administration-s-ties

"Symbol," en.wikipedia.org/wiki/Symbol

"The Value of Wisdom in Politics," by Arizona's 19th Governor, Fife Symington III (Republican) and Arizona's 54th Speaker of the House, Russell "Rusty" Bowers (Republican), from *Prop 140 Freedom Times*, November 2024—General Election Edition, Prop140.com.

"Timeline of Trump's Coronavirus Responses," Blog Post, doggett. house.gov, March 22, 2022.

"Trump's election order could boot thousands from voting," in "Your Turn," by Stephen Richer, *Arizona Republic,* March 29, 2025.

"Trump refuses to accept election results, says it's 'far from over'," by Kevin Breuninger, Politics, *CNBC News,* November 7, 2020.

twitter.com/thedailybeast/status/1337447080537845762 for The Daily Beast on X: "Protesters shared Arizona House Speaker Rust… these were members of his own party."

"Update on Forensic Audit of Maricopa County's Tabulation Equipment," from Scott Jarrett, Director of Election Day and Emergency Voting, and Rey Valenzuela, Director of Election Services and Early Voting, to the Maricopa County Board of Supervisors, February 23, 2021.

"UPDATES: Election Info & COVID-19," content.govdelivery.com/ accounts/AZMARIC/bulletins/186468b
with Message from Supervisor Gates, March 13, 2020.

United States Election Assistance Commission, "Help America Vote Act," eac.gov/about/help_america_vote_act.aspx

"US election: Full transcript of Donald Trump's obscene videotape," BBC, October 9, 2016.

"What is a metaphor, grade 5?" en.wikipedia.org/wiki/Metaphor

"Yes, Virginia, there is a Santa Claus," en.wikipedia.org/wiki/Yes,_ Virginia,_there_is_a_ Santa_Claus

en.wikipedia.org/wiki/2020_United_States_presidential_election_in_ Arizona, "2020 United States presidential election in Arizona."

Videos

"Congressional Hearing" oversightdemocrats.house.gov/sites/evo-subsites/democrats-oversight.house.gov/files/Gates%20Testimony.pdf

washingtonpost.com/video/politics/clint-hickman-faced-death-threats-for-telling-the-truth/2021/10/31/6d22d0cc-0f08-40e9-84c0-c6493ee0731d_video.html

c-span.org/program/house-committee/house-hearing-on-arizona-2020-election-audit/603697

oversightdemocrats.house.gov/legislation/hearings/assessing-the-election-audit-in-arizona-and-threats-to-american-democracy

youtube.com/live/XUHPaJWiG68 for Maricopa County BOS Special Meeting to Canvass the 2020 Election, November 20, 2020.

youtube.com/watch?v=hsT15qLqkAg for "I'm sorry, I can't do this," *FOX 10 Phoenix,* Scott Jarrett, the Maricopa County, Arizona Election Day Director, walks away from podium during a news briefing regarding the March 17 Presidential Preference Election, March 13, 2020.

ABOUT THE AUTHOR

Nancy Hicks Marshall grew up in a Republican household. She always appreciated the caution with which her parents viewed spending, and her father's recognition that government regulation was sometimes necessary to "keep the foxes from the henhouse." Didn't they support law, order, and civil discourse? Thus, she was shocked when two Republican legislators and the County Supervisors were threatened, insulted, doxxed, vilified, and even SWATTED by extremist right-wing Republicans during the 2020 election.

Since childhood, Marshall has disliked the abuse of power. In 2009, she defended a young man who was unconstitutionally jailed in the auditorium of the Maricopa County Board of Supervisors for exercising his First Amendment rights—clapping after a speaker, then sitting quietly upon request. That successful defense led to *A Dry Hate*, a multiple award-winning novel, covering the time in Arizona history when a popular Sheriff jailed or "investigated" activists, brown people, and political opponents at will.

A practicing attorney for many years, followed by a career in writing, Marshall has returned to the Maricopa County Board of Supervisors with *Six Who Stopped the Steal*—perhaps not what you think it was. Drawing on intimate in-person accounts from the six men, a conversation about "monsters," a detailed chronology of the 2020 elections, and the words of the six themselves, Marshall offers us insight into the courage and integrity of men whose actions prevented the steal of the 2020 elections in Arizona by unscrupulous extremists.

Marshall has authored *A Rattler's Tale, Un Cuento de Una Serpiente de Cascabel* (the Spanish translation of *Rattler*), *Finding Zachariah in a Community Garden*, and *A Dry Hate*.